Is Your Child Depressed?

Answers to Your Toughest Questions

NATHAN NAPARSTEK, PH.D.

WITH MARILYN WALLACE

McGraw·Hill

New York   Chicago   San Francisco   Lisbon   London   Madrid   Mexico City
Milan   New Delhi   San Juan   Seoul   Singapore   Sydney   Toronto

The *McGraw·Hill* Companies

Library of Congress Cataloging-in-Publication Data

Naparstek, Nathan.
 Is your child depressed? : answers to your toughest questions / Nathan Naparstek with
Marilyn Wallace.
    p.   cm.
 Includes bibliographical references and index.
 ISBN 0-07-145756-9
    1. Depression in children.   2. Depression in adolescence.   3. Affective disorders in
children.   4. Parenting.   I. Wallace, Marilyn.   II. Title.

RJ506.D4N37   2005
618.92'8527—dc22   2005010298

1 2 3 4 5 6 7 8 9 0 FGR/FGR 0 9 8 7 6 5

ISBN 0-07-145756-9

McGraw-Hill books are available at special quantity discounts to use as premiums and sales
promotions, or for use in corporate training programs. For more information, please write to the
Director of Special Sales, Professional Publishing, McGraw-Hill, Two Penn Plaza, New York, NY
10121-2298. Or contact your local bookstore.

This book is printed on acid-free paper.

Contents

12 Behavior Management 195

13 Positive Communication 207

14 Moving Toward a Better Future 219

    Resources 233

    Bibliography 235

    Index 237

Acknowledgments

THANK YOU TO Jane Dystel for recognizing the importance of this book, as well as to Michele Matrisciani, my editor at McGraw-Hill, for her enthusiasm and assistance. I also want to thank Miriam Goderich and Jessica Papin at Dystel & Goderich Literary Management. They did more than just represent me, providing intensive assistance in the initial editing of the book. They also connected me with my collaborator on this book, Marilyn Wallace, who not only provided great suggestions but was also a pleasure to work with. In addition, I want to thank Michael Bourret for handling the final arrangements of getting the book out.

I want to thank my friend and colleague Dr. Ed Burke for taking time to review early drafts of my work and, as always, my wife, Denise, who has read countless versions of my writings and is my number one partner plus proofreader. I also want to thank my children, Eli, Rachel, and Joey, for their time and patience with me while I have been busy writing and counseling patients, as well as for understanding the need to kick them off the computer when I had writing to do.

Most of all, I want to thank the children and families I have seen in counseling for giving me the opportunity to work with you. It is an honor to have been let into your lives and to have earned your trust.

Introduction

WHEN ANGELA CALLED to make an appointment for me to see her fourteen-year-old daughter, Gina, she sounded exasperated and concerned. Why was Gina, previously a B+ student, failing almost all of her classes? To make matters worse, mother and daughter were fighting all the time. Perhaps Gina had gotten in with the wrong crowd, her mother suggested, or maybe she was entering that dreaded stage of adolescent rebellion she'd heard so much about.

But when I met with Gina, a slender young woman with a pretty but unsmiling face, she told me that she was "just sad." Gina couldn't remember the last time she'd felt truly happy. Eventually, with downcast eyes and a barely audible voice, she admitted that she spent part of every day crying and had withdrawn from all her favorite pastimes. She avoided seeing friends because she hated "putting on an act" by feigning interest in their activities and conversations. She could no longer get a good night's rest, which made her tired and irritable all the time. Although she fought frequently with her mother, Gina didn't want to upset her and thus kept her feelings of hopelessness and despair to herself.

Until the day she arrived in my office, Gina had suffered in silence. Although Angela was aware that she and Gina were fighting a lot and that Gina's grades had plummeted, she was surprised when I diagnosed her daughter with depression. Even Angela, an attentive parent, had missed the warning signs, in part because she had such a hard time acknowledging that her child was unhappy. However, once the diagnosis was made, Angela ceased to take Gina's irritability personally. She understood that Gina wasn't trying to be uncooperative and unpleasant but instead suffered from a condition that needed treatment.

Gina and her mother continued to see me every other week for six months. Together, we worked on building strategies to improve Gina's ability to deal with stress and conflict, as well as ways to enhance her self-esteem and communication skills. Little by little, Gina began to feel more confident. She started enjoying time with her friends again and described feeling happy for the first time in years. We also worked in concert with her teachers, who, alerted to her special needs, gave her extra help and understanding. As a result, her grades went back up. By collaborating with Gina's family and key people at her school to address her needs, we were able to treat her depression successfully.

Is Your Child Depressed? is designed to serve as a guidebook, a tool to help parents and other concerned adults navigate the unfamiliar landscape of childhood depression. My goal is to help parents, educators, youth workers, and others identify and understand depression, as well as gain insight into what childhood depression is and how it is diagnosed and treated. But equally important, I want to share with parents the practical strategies for negotiating the unique—and considerable—day-to-day challenges of living with a depressed child. I've developed these strategies with the help of all the families I've worked with as school psychologist and in private practice over the past two decades, and have seen them work so well that I'm pleased to have the opportunity to make them available to as many families as possible.

So, what can you expect from this book?

You will learn how to differentiate depression from ordinary sadness, create a home environment that will support a child's healing, and get the right kind of outside assistance from professionals, including doctors, psychologists, and teachers. You will get tips on how to better communicate and resolve conflicts with a depressed child, work effectively with the school system, and deal with the family problems that depression generates. Because he or she already has an "I don't care" attitude, a depressed child is less likely to respond to behavior management strategies that are successful with the average child, so new ways to confront the knotty problem of discipline will be explored.

Parents will also learn what to expect in the counseling process and will develop a better understanding of the medications used to treat depression's symptoms. The controversy over the use of antidepressant medications in treating childhood depression raises many questions that parents must address. I hope you find the discussions in Chapters 5, 6, and 7 informative. I've included guidelines for determining when drugs might be used, monitoring children for side effects, and withdrawing children from a drug regimen. Information changes almost daily, so I urge parents to keep informed about the latest medical findings.

Most of all, I want to instill in every parent who reads this book a feeling that things can get better. It won't happen by magic, and it won't happen all at once, but with adequate information, an open heart, and diligence, parents can help their children achieve a happier, more productive future.

▼

PART I

Reading the Signs
Understanding Childhood Depression

- ▶ How can I tell if my child is depressed?
- ▶ How is childhood depression different from adult depression?
- ▶ What causes depression?
- ▶ What's the relationship between genetic and environmental factors?
- ▶ Are all depressions alike?
- ▶ How is childhood depression diagnosed?
- ▶ How can I prepare for an initial interview with a mental health professional?
- ▶ What will happen in the initial interview?
- ▶ What if I think my child is at risk to commit suicide?

1

Characteristics of Childhood Depression

UNDERSTANDING CHILDHOOD DEPRESSION is an important first step in helping your child. As your child's best advocate, the more you know, the more effective you can be. The case histories throughout this book not only illustrate what depression is and how to treat it, they also provide real-life examples of children and their families coping with depression.

What Is Childhood Depression?

When Billy first stepped into my office, he was fourteen years old and on the verge of trouble. He awoke each morning dreading the thought of school and longing to avoid the endless stresses of getting there, being there, and coping with the demands of interacting with teachers and classmates. He was so tired he could only shuffle from one activity to the next, unable to concentrate on anything his teachers said. No way could he get his work done, which added the twin burdens of guilt and shame about his poor academic performance to his troubles. He cried almost every night and dissolved into tears over the tiniest of problems. Every parental request to do his homework or to help around the house was treated as a major imposition, and he snapped at his startled mom and dad to leave him alone. Billy hated himself and believed he was a burden to his family. Even though he was a handsome child, with long-lashed brown eyes and regular features, he felt that he was ugly and was convinced that no girl would ever like him. Watching television and playing video games became his daily escape. By the time he was midway through ninth grade, Billy had decided that he was a bad person because he had such negative feelings, and he assumed that everyone else felt the same way about him.

Billy was one of the approximately four to six million American children suffering from depression. The National Institute of Mental Health, the federal agency for research on mental health and behavior disorders, estimates that one in ten children suffers from mental illness severe enough to cause impairment. The U.S. Department of Health and Human Services estimates that up to 15 percent of children and adolescents exhibit mental health problems. Whichever statistic you use as a yardstick, the number is distressingly high.

Depression in Children May Not Look Like Adult Depression

When most people think about depression, they usually picture a gloomy, dispirited Sad Sack walking through life like the cartoon character who carries his own dark cloud wherever he goes. But depression may look very different in children than it does in adults. Instead of sitting quietly in his room and crying, a child may yell, scream, use foul language, be defiant, and throw temper tantrums. Children tend to exhibit depression by displaying anger and irritability, especially with family members. When they're at home, depressed children might argue with parents, pick fights with siblings, or become annoyed at requests to help around the house. Children who are depressed try to avoid doing things that make them feel more irritable, such as chores or homework. Moreover, it's unlikely that a child will be able to tell anyone that she's feeling depressed.

Depression Is Not a Choice That a Child Makes

Depression is something that happens to a child—it is not a choice. Childhood depression appears to be associated with a biochemical imbalance in the brain that leads to negative changes in a child's mood, attitude, energy level, sleep, concentration, appetite, self-esteem, social relationships, family life, and school performance.

Children who are depressed may behave in ways that test the patience of parents, teachers, siblings, and friends, but they aren't simply being willful and difficult. Depression is an unwanted illness that in no way reflects upon the moral character of a child. Some of the kindest and most wonderful children I have worked with in my twenty-four years as a school psychologist and sixteen years of private therapy practice have suffered from its symptoms. What all those children have taught me is that depression is a serious illness that affects a child's ability to meet the demands of his or her life situation.

Being angry and irritable is not a natural state for a child. I've heard depression described as anger turned inward, but there's a limit to how much anger a person can keep inside before he lets it out on other people. When parents ask me why their child is so angry, they seem to be thinking that if they knew who or what provoked such strong feelings in their child, they could fix everything. What they don't yet understand is that too many problems can't be solved by a simple conversation because the problems are really manifestations of depression.

No child would voluntarily choose to be so unhappy and cut off from the satisfactions of ordinary life for long periods of time. And no parent who struggles to make sense of a child's difficult and even provocative behavior in the midst of the responsibilities of jobs, school, and family wants that child to be miserable when something can be done to help. The first step in getting the right help for a child is to understand depression, where it comes from, what it looks like, and what treatments and strategies exist to help alleviate its symptoms.

Why Do Children Become Depressed?

Depression, like so many other experiences that are part of the human condition, appears to be a function of a combination of genetic and environmental factors.

Although some researchers have noted that peak times for the onset of depression are November and May, they don't fully understand the link between the changing seasons and depression. A more complete explanation of what causes someone to become depressed includes a genetic predisposition and an environmental trigger. Depression has complex origins and appears to be associated with a person's ability to deal with stress. Children inherit a predisposition for how stress is handled. Yet some children live in chaotic, unstable environments and don't become depressed, while others who grow up in wonderfully calm and secure families succumb to depression. Neither factor taken by itself is a reliable predictor of whether a child will become depressed.

The Gene Factor

Studies show that a susceptibility to depression is inherited. If a parent has experienced depression, a 25 percent probability exists that a child will also suffer from its symptoms. It's important to remember, however, that the majority of depressed parents don't have depressed children. Parents who have had direct and personal experience with depression shouldn't assume that their children will follow in their footsteps.

Still, the notion of a genetic predisposition toward depression has a pretty strong basis in scientific study. The concordance rate of identical twins (the rate at which both twins experience depression) is approximately 75 percent. For fraternal twins, the concordance rate is about 25 percent. The significantly higher rate of depression among identical twins versus fraternal twins is strong evidence of a genetic component.

Over the years that I've worked with families and children, I've discovered that several members of a family may exhibit similar symptoms. When a parent also suffers from depression, treatment for the child can be complicated. A depressed parent can barely tread water and may lack the energy to care adequately for a child with problems, no matter how much she loves him. In this situation, the depressed parent needs to seek treatment for herself before she can be of significant help to her child.

Simply having a genetic predisposition may not, by itself, be enough to ensure that a child will become depressed. Hormonal changes during puberty, the stress of high expectations that can't be met, traumatic events, or even the daily demands of interacting with peers or family members can all trigger depression. Sometimes, however, the origin of depression is nearly impossible to identify.

▶ **What Triggered Tammy's Depression?**

Tammy, a seven-year-old girl, was referred to me by her pediatrician. She was a good student who lived in a stable, loving home with both her biological parents. No trauma had visited her young life, no loss had befallen her, and she had no visible reason to feel unhappy and depressed. Yet her former enthusiasm for school and for her weekly horseback riding and dancing lessons had disappeared, and she talked frequently about wanting to die.

Tammy's mother, Leslie, told me that although Tammy had always been an anxious child, her constant feelings of sadness were only about a month old. Neither Tammy nor her parents understood why she was suddenly overcome by despair. However, her parents reported that while they themselves were not currently depressed, both their families had a strong history of depression. My best guess was that a genetic predisposition for depression was being manifested, although the trigger was unknown.

During my initial counseling session, I offered Leslie strategies to help Tammy feel better. We talked about helping her to exchange negative thoughts for more positive ones and discussed outlets (such as writing in a diary and painting) that would encourage her to share her feelings. I also suggested that her parents actively listen to Tammy's feelings without judging them.

Leslie called me prior to the second session and noted that Tammy's negative feelings had become more intense. When I saw Tammy, I found that her depression had, in fact, become worse. She was spending all her time in her room, and all she did was sleep and cry. More disturbing, she reported having constant thoughts about hurting herself, although she hadn't developed any plans to carry out her fantasies.

I called Tammy's pediatrician to recommend that we start her on a very small dose of antidepressant medication. Medicating any child for depression is not a simple decision, and I only suggest that when it seems necessary. Some medications have serious side effects. Friends and family members may tease a child for taking medication, or they may worry and be overprotective. A child on medication may feel there's something terribly wrong with her, thereby reinforcing her own lack of self-esteem. The decision to put a child on medication should be made only after counseling strategies have proven ineffective and a child is still depressed or when the depression appears to be worsening in severity.

I almost always advise that children start on the smallest dose possible, since they can be susceptible to the medication's side effects. Tammy's pediatrician suggested a daily dose of 25 mg of Zoloft, but I felt that an even smaller dose, 12.5 mg, was appropriate. After several weeks, during which Tammy's parents closely monitored her behavior, her dosage was increased to 25 mg.

The Medication Question. When a child seems to have a strong genetic tendency toward depression, the likelihood is greater that medications will become part of her treatment. The use of antidepressant medication, much in the news, is so important that I've set aside a separate chapter for a more complete discussion. In Chapter 5, I'll try to make sense of the confusing maze of medication information. Some researchers maintain that antidepressant medications may make things worse and not better for children. The U.S. Food and Drug Administration (FDA) has recently required drug companies to clearly specify to consumers that antidepressant medications (specifically SSRIs [selective serotonin reuptake inhibitors], such as Paxil, Prozac, Zoloft, Celexa, and Lexapro) may have unwanted side effects (for example, anxiety, insomnia, irritability, severe restlessness, and worsening depression and suicidal ideation) in both adults and children. But the FDA also reviewed several studies of the use of antidepressants with children and found that no suicides had been reported. What's a parent to do?

The first thing I advise is that parents be cautious and observant. There is no need to panic and discontinue medication for a child if he isn't showing signs of side effects. In fact, the abrupt withdrawal of medications may be harmful. Much evidence, both in research and in the experiences of people who treat children for depression, shows that many children do benefit from the use of medication—*so long as they are properly monitored by physicians and mental health professionals.*

By its nature, depression carries with it the potential for suicidal thoughts and feelings. Suicidal ideation may develop in the course of a depression, even when no medication has been used in treatment. Suicidal thoughts, then, can be a correlative effect of the depression itself instead of a causal effect of the medication.

This is one case in which statistics may lead to confusion. Imagine saying that eating ice cream leads people to commit murder! But a positive statistical relationship exists between ice cream consumption and murders in New York City. Both rise in the summer months. The difference between correlation and causality is clear: eating ice cream doesn't cause people to commit murder, even though reports show that people eat more ice cream in the summer and also commit more homicides then.

The real problem, as I see it, is that once children are placed on antidepressant medication, they may not be adequately monitored. It's easy for a doctor to prescribe medication but not quite so easy to be vigilant for signs of agitation or poor impulse control. Sometimes doctors can't be easily reached when a parent has concerns. Perhaps parent and doctor haven't made arrangements to check in at frequent and appropriate intervals to see how a child is responding to medication. Only informed parents can ensure that their child is properly monitored while taking antidepressant medication.

For Tammy, a child from a happy and well-adjusted family, whose depression had no apparent cause, the combination of medication and counseling helped her step out from under that dark cloud. She learned to incorporate the strategies we'd discussed in counseling for changing negative thoughts into positive ones. At my suggestion, she also added a daily exercise routine. Being busy seemed to help her avoid negative feelings. As it is with so many other children, a properly managed course of treatment that combined counseling and medication was effective in treating Tammy's depression. Without the medication, she probably wouldn't have made as quick a recovery, and without the counseling, she wouldn't have learned strategies to combat her negative feelings.

After six months, Tammy was weaned off her medication and continued to thrive and do quite well without it. Currently she is free of any symptoms of depression. Tammy's parents were made aware of signs that the depression might be reactivating, and I made sure they knew that Tammy should come see me for periodic checkups, particularly if they suspected that she was experiencing a relapse. Any child who has experienced major depression should be carefully monitored for signs that something is amiss. Untreated depression frequently comes back, and after a single bout of depression, there is about a 50 percent chance of recurrence. The more frequent the incidence, the greater the risk that the depression will return.

The Environment Factor

Traumatic events seem to have triggered depression in other children I have worked with. Loss of a loved one, witnessing violence, or being the victim of physical or sexual abuse are among the events that place a child at significant risk for experiencing symptoms of depression.

▶ **What Was Happening in Steven's Life?**

Steven, an eleven-year-old boy, was referred to me by his pediatrician because he wasn't listening to his mother and was failing most of his sixth-grade classes. This frustrating situation had been building for several months. Steven and his younger sister, Melissa, lived with their mother, Grace, who had been married for about a year to their stepfather, Alan. Steven had been a well-behaved child until about six months before I began seeing him. Now, he spent endless hours alone in his room and never actively sought out his friends. He put little effort into his schoolwork, didn't study for tests, and neglected his homework. Grace tried talking to Steven, but he was unresponsive, and she remained mystified by his behavior.

Although I'd suggested that it would be helpful for both parents to be present, only Steven and Grace came for the first appointment. Alan refused to participate, saying that he didn't want any part of family counseling. For me, that was like a blinking neon arrow pointing to problems in the family relationships. During that visit, Steven exhibited what is commonly called a blank affect. He didn't smile; his facial expression remained the same no matter what we talked about. When I gave him the Child Depression Inventory, a depression scale for elementary school–aged children, he scored at the moderate to high level.

I decided that my initial approach with Steven would be to break the cycle of negative interactions by sharing with him and Grace some of the strategies I've developed over the years for changing how parent and child communicate and for how discipline is handled. I recommended that Grace ease up on her punishments, since they were having little effect. I also suggested that she set aside special time to talk and interact with Steven, when she could give him her undivided attention. As discussed in Chapters 12 and 13, I assured Grace that these strategies don't require a specialized degree in psychology but are, instead, simple tools for making small changes in daily living that can have a powerful impact.

During the second visit, I spent most of my time alone with Steven. Among other things, I asked him how he got along with his stepfather. I waited quietly for Steven's words, but instead tears made their way down his clenched face. When he was finally ready to speak, he reported that his stepfather beat him regularly, whenever Grace was out of the house. Steven said that Alan had even punched him in the head. And when he wasn't hitting him, Alan yelled at him and belittled him. Not surprisingly, Steven was afraid of his stepfather.

I told Steven that I would have to share this information with his mother, and I immediately called her into my office. Grace had noticed her son's bruises, but Steven had told her that they were the result of bicycle accidents. Grace was horrified to hear that Alan was hitting her son. And she was anguished because she had been unaware of the problem and therefore had done nothing to stop it. Steven had suffered in silence because he was afraid that if he said anything, Alan would get so angry that he'd hurt him even more.

Gently, I informed Grace that Alan's behavior constituted child abuse and I was obligated to report it to the Department of Social Services. Furious with her husband for hurting Steven and anxious to protect her son, Grace assured me that she had no problem with this.

A caseworker went to the home the next day, and Alan admitted to the abuse. Even though Grace was in a difficult financial situation, she decided to take Steven and Melissa and move out of what had been the family home.

During our next visit, I saw Steven smile for the first time. He no longer had a blank affect. He seemed lighter, more engaged, more relaxed. He felt safe in his home for the first time in months and had begun to come out of his shell. Alan refused to get treatment for his anger control issues; he and Grace permanently separated. The separation wasn't a problem for Steven, now a happy child who could play with his friends and concentrate enough to do well in school.

When a child is depressed, it is important to be aware that potential underlying causes, such as abuse, might be factors. While most depressed children haven't been abused, treating a child for depression and never dealing with its root cause would be both ineffective and harmful. Abused children may be afraid to talk about what's happening to them because they've been threatened with severe consequences. Abusive situations can go undetected, or at least unreported, for years.

The first priority must be to remove the child from danger. A parent who suspects that her child has been abused should let him know that she will protect him, no matter who has hurt him. A child's depression can't be successfully treated if he feels unsafe or threatened. Being in an abusive situation can have long-term negative effects on a child's mental and physical health and needs to be addressed by calling the local child protective agency or the National Child Abuse Hotline at 800-422-4453.

From Toddler to Teen

It's important for parents to understand what childhood depression is and to learn to recognize its signs. One of the first things parents should know is that depression may look different in younger children than it does in adolescents.

Despite considerable evidence to the contrary, some people still refuse to believe that young children can get depressed. In the 1950s, many psychologists, especially those working within a psychoanalytic model, believed that young children couldn't become depressed. This misconception prevented many children from receiving effective, timely, and appropriate treatment for their problems.

Even Very Young Children Can Be Depressed

If I could, I would have introduced the skeptics to Susan, who came to my office and talked incessantly about her "bad feeling." Susan had lost interest in her favorite activities, stopped playing with her friends, and told her parents that she wanted to be dead. She'd spent more time in the school nurse's office than in her classroom.

Susan was six years old and suffering from depression. Proper treatment helped Susan recover. Without it, she might still be an unhappy child, alone and in pain.

The risk for depression does tend to increase as we grow older. Depression in infants is rare but real. Rene Spitz, a noted psychological researcher, found that infants who were in an institutional orphanage after World War II refused to eat and eventually died if they weren't held by their caretakers. Children have an innate need to be held and comforted. If those needs aren't met, then even very young children can fail to thrive and may become sick and die.

Approximately 1 percent of preschoolers experience depression; they often have great difficulty articulating their feelings because their language skills aren't sufficiently developed. Instead of verbalizing feelings, the depressed preschool child is likely to show emotions by exhibiting significant aggressive, noncompliant, irritable, fearful, whiny, or crying behavior. While most preschool children get irritable if they're hungry or sleepy, may be afraid when their parents go away, and may even stomp their feet and whine to try to get Daddy to buy them the latest toy, these behaviors are often carried to extremes of intensity and frequency in depressed children.

Although a diagnosis of clinical depression is rare in preschool children, there are times when it is appropriate. In most cases, the child has experienced significant trauma resulting from the death or absence of a parent, has witnessed or been the victim of violence, or has had a significant health problem that has interrupted normal emotional or physical development. I find preschool children to be more resilient than older children in dealing with these events, as long as they have a supportive parent and receive treatment soon after the precipitating event.

According to a 1999 surgeon general's report, up to 5 percent of elementary school–aged children become depressed. With children aged six to twelve, typical behaviors that accompany depression include greater irritability, more frequent and more severe incidence of behavior problems, stomachache or headache complaints, and problems with being alone or separating from a parent.

Adolescence: Rebellion, Hormones, Depression

As youngsters move toward adolescence, the incidence of depression is estimated in the surgeon general's report to increase to at least 10 percent of children. With children twelve to seventeen years old, the complaints that lead their parents to seek treatment for them are likely to be withdrawal, fatigue, a generally sad demeanor, and the increased possibility of drug or alcohol abuse. Parents may actually have more of an opportunity to become aware of depression in older children because they are more capable of expressing their feelings.

In my role as counselor and therapist, I've come to believe that simply going through puberty and adolescence can be a trigger. A child who is experiencing major changes in hormone levels and body shape is a child under stress. Testosterone and estrogen and their powerful effects on teen sexuality and skin conditions can play havoc with emotions and with the finely tuned chemistry of the body and the brain.

As an adolescent's emotional reactions become more intense, a predisposition to depression may become manifest. A specific event— for example, a major illness, an accident, a breakup with a boyfriend or girlfriend, physical or sexual abuse, being bullied, being excluded by peers, moving, or losing a friend or family member—may also cause the onset of depression. If a child is already on overload and can't handle a single additional problem, even a relatively minor event may spark an episode of depression.

Before puberty, any difference in the incidence of depression in boys and in girls is negligible. After puberty, however, girls appear to experience depression twice as often. There are several possible explanations for this finding. The hormonal changes girls go through during puberty and the onset of menstruation may play a role in depression. Another factor may be that adolescent girls are more willing to discuss and report feelings of depression than are boys of the same age. Cultural factors that make girls more susceptible to depression as they get older, such as pressures to conform to current notions of attractiveness and unrealistic expectations that they will be sweet and cooperative simply because they are girls, may also play a role.

Whatever their ages, children who are depressed behave in ways that let a parent know that something is wrong. While parents shouldn't worry that every episode of sadness signals a serious problem, it's important to recognize and understand signs that might indicate that it's time to seek help for a child from a medical or mental health professional.

Recognizing Childhood Depression

Too many children suffering from the symptoms of depression will never be identified, and they won't receive the treatment they need and deserve. Many parents have come to my office not knowing that their children had been clinically depressed until months or even years after the initial symptoms appeared. Yet if they had known what to look for, these parents would certainly have sought help for their children.

Measuring children by the same yardstick we use for adults is one of the problems—a depressed child may seem cranky and rebellious at home, yet her withdrawn behavior in school may send a signal that a teacher can't interpret properly. Aggressive or hyperactive children are sure to attract the notice of teachers, while the shy, quiet child may not get the attention she desperately needs.

When a teacher does make a referral to a psychologist, it's usually because a child is misbehaving and disturbing the class. A child who jumps out of his seat every five minutes, interrupts the teacher in the middle of a lesson, frequently fights with peers, and talks back to school staff is likely to be referred to a psychologist. The child who is hurting inside but isn't bothering anyone else is often ignored, even though he may be in severe emotional distress. While depressed children may exhibit behavioral difficulties in the school setting, their symptoms tend to be more covert and are more difficult for adults to notice. Because depressed children tend to feel less secure at school than they do at home, they're more likely to avoid getting negative attention from teachers and administrators.

▶ **How Serious Was John's Depression?**

Seven-year-old John was referred to my private practice by his pediatrician. He lived with his mother, Alice, and ten-year-old sister, Rebecca, and had little contact with his biological father. He was a very unhappy child—friendless, irritable, and doing poorly in school. His mother sought help after she'd become increasingly alarmed because he talked frequently about killing himself, both at home and in school.

I gave John the Child Depression Inventory, and he scored in the extremely depressed range. He didn't see anything good in his life. He hated everyone, including himself. He didn't enjoy doing anything. Of greatest concern to me was John's declaration that he wanted to kill himself. When asked how he would do this, John had a detailed plan prepared: he would go into the middle of his street and run up to a car and make sure it hit him.

Until that moment, nobody had talked to John about his feelings so directly, and nobody knew just how distressed he was. As our session continued, John ceased to be nasty and defiant. Instead, he appeared to be relieved that, finally, he had shared his feelings. I thanked John for his honesty and let him know that I was concerned about him and that I had to talk to his mother about what he had said.

When Alice came back into my office, I told her that I felt John wasn't safe. I recommended that she take him to a psychiatric hospital for a placement evaluation. John was admitted for a hospital stay that lasted a month, typical for a child with depressed and suicidal symptoms. While in the hospital, he received intensive therapy and was prescribed 20 mg of Prozac.

John was so transformed when he went back to school five weeks later that his teacher could hardly believe he was the same child. He was polite and friendly to her and the other students. Alice reported that for the first time she could remember, she truly enjoyed spending time with her son. No longer burdened by the misery of his suicidal feelings, John could manifest his positive qualities.

We continued to do counseling and developed exercises that encouraged John to express his feelings instead of bottling them up. His medication needed to be adjusted periodically, and there were still ups and downs. But we had a workable situation, and John was no longer at risk of killing himself.

Left untreated, John could have been a tragedy in the making.

Signs of Depression

Most people don't know how to recognize depression in children. John had many of the signs: he was sad, irritable, angry, alienated from other children, and doing poorly in school. But it was only his talk of killing himself that got the attention of his mother and his pediatrician. He'd been suffering from severe depression for a full year before his suicidal symptoms led to treatment.

Living with depression is, in many ways, more painful for a child than suffering from a physical injury. A child with a broken leg has a wound that everyone can see and a cast that friends can sign as a means of expressing their concern. Instead of having an obvious boo-boo, depressed children often seem to be wearing an invisible sign that reads, "I'm unhappy. Don't bother me." Even though they may communicate a nonverbal message that says, "Keep away," children suffering from depression are desperate to have people care about them and offer the comfort of support.

A child is unlikely to come to his father after dinner one evening and say that he is suffering from depression. But a parent who knows what to look for can recognize signs that a child is experiencing something more troublesome than just a bad day.

Attitudes and Feelings of Depressed Children

Many depressed children exhibit similar attitudes that reflect emotions of hopelessness and self-blame. Their behavior may be seen as delivering messages about their depression.

I don't care. Some of the signs of depression are a pervasive "I don't care" attitude and significant changes in behavior. A child experiencing symptoms of depression usually has difficulty completing assigned tasks both at home and at school and has cut himself off from friends and family. He is no longer interested in things that used to be important to him.

I can't do it. One of the most observable characteristics of depression is a lack of energy, which may be accompanied by a change in eating or sleeping patterns. A depressed child might have trouble getting up in the morning, come late to school, be constantly tired, or even fall asleep in class. She often looks tired and accomplishes a lot less than she used to. Her concentration tends to be impaired, and she has difficulty making decisions. A depressed child may become so absorbed by her negative feelings and thoughts that she can't pay attention to schoolwork at all. It's important to realize that this lack of concentration is not deliberate and is very often a source of further distress to the child. I've heard over and over again from the children I see, both in school and in private practice, how upset they are about not being able to complete work in school or concentrate at home.

I won't try that. A child who exhibits symptoms of depression tends to be rigid and inflexible, not only in his ability to solve problems but also in many other aspects of his life. It's hard for him to deal effectively with changes in his daily routines. Depressed people are seldom easygoing. A depressed child is likely to have low self-esteem and make many negative comments about himself and others. Not surprisingly, the cycle of bad feelings leads to behavior that gets a negative response, and this adds to the tension.

It's all my fault. What a healthy person perceives as a little problem may be a traumatic event to a depressed child. It's important not to impose adult interpretations and values on the experiences of a depressed child. She sees the world as a dark and unhappy place where bad things keep happening to her. Sometimes she might take ownership of problems when, in fact, she's done nothing to cause them. Depressed children, particularly younger ones, are hard on themselves in part because they tend to feel that they have more control over a situation than they really do. A young child may even blame herself for her parents' divorce. She's convinced that if she'd been a better child, her parents wouldn't have split up. Many

Signs of Depression

It's not always easy to recognize the signs of depression in children, especially since some of the same behaviors may simply indicate that a child has had a bad day. But if your child has experienced three or more of the following symptoms to a significant degree for several weeks, he or she may be depressed.

Sadness

- Complains about being unhappy
- Frequently cries
- Does not take pleasure in things

Problems with Sleep

- Sleeps too much
- Has difficulty falling asleep
- Frequently wakes up at night
- Has difficulty getting up in the morning

Changes in Peer Relationships

- Avoids getting together with old friends
- Has new friends who seem to have a lot of problems
- Frequently complains about how other children treat him

Low Energy

- Always seems tired
- Doesn't seem to get things done like he or she used to
- Doesn't participate in activities like he or she used to
- Avoids engaging in activities that require effort

New Difficulties in Concentration

- Complains about being unable to concentrate
- Spends less time on things that used to be of interest
- Doesn't seem to be listening when spoken to

Recent Decline in School Performance

- Does poorly on tests
- Does less well than usual in school grades
- Spends less time than usual on homework
- Exhibits a decline in school behavior

Irritability

- Directs more mean-tempered remarks toward others than usual
- Lacks patience with parents or siblings
- Has significantly more difficulty dealing with negative events
- Yells and screams at others often
- Is easily frustrated

Pessimism

- Talks about the future being hopeless
- Expects to fail or do poorly
- Makes frequent negative comments about herself

Negative Body Language

- Rarely seems to smile or laugh anymore
- Seems to have lost his sense of humor
- Has little facial expression when spoken to
- Frequently walks with his head down

Changes in Eating Routine

- Eats a lot less than usual
- Eats significantly more and has gained a lot of unneeded weight
- Does not sit down to eat meals with the family anymore

Suicidal Comments or Self-Abusive Behavior

- Talks about wanting to be dead
- Is obsessed with death in art and music
- Makes cuts on her body

depressed children have expressed great relief when they realize that the bad things happening in their lives aren't their fault.

Patterns of Behavior in Depressed Children

Changes in everyday behavior may indicate to parents that they should consider that their child might be experiencing depression. But other signals may be more difficult to spot because they are patterns of behavior that may have more subtle manifestations, and these bear special attention.

Negative View of the Future. Erin's parents often admonished her about her poor grades, warning that she would never get into a good college if she didn't work harder. They often did this during car rides, when she was unable to run away to her room and close her door. Many conversations turned into shouting matches; Erin and her parents never had a productive conversation regarding her grades and her future. Her parents didn't know that Erin was depressed.

Like Erin, children who are depressed don't have a positive view of the future and tend to feel that things are hopeless. I think of them as future impaired. They're so preoccupied with their negative moods that they have difficulty accepting the possibility of long-term rewards. A depressed adolescent often sees little point in working toward future goals and has difficulty making decisions that might relate to college or vocational aspirations, in part because she's so focused on the struggle to get through the current day.

Understandably, this can be a frustrating experience for parents trying to guide a child toward a happy, fulfilled, and successful life. Yet the more the parents try to get their child to address long-term issues, the angrier the child becomes because she's convinced she can't measure up to her parents' expectations. How distressing to realize that the more you try to connect with your child, the more you turn her away! But parents who are aware of their child's depression can break the cycle and truly connect with their child.

Parents can help a child who has a negative view of the future by keeping her connected to the immediate present. In Chapters 10 and 14, I'll discuss several strategies to help parents encourage their children to get beyond "future impairment" and create and sustain a more positive perception of the future.

Feelings of Helplessness. Adam was an eleven-year-old whose parents brought him to see me because he was doing poorly in school and felt sad all the time. Whenever they gave him suggestions for improving his situation, he cried and repeatedly told them that their proposed solution wouldn't do any good. Adam felt helpless in the face of his depression.

Just telling Adam that things were better than he imagined and that he should ditch his dim view of things wouldn't have done a thing to help him feel better. Such a conscious shift in mind-set is difficult for a depressed child. He simply cannot look on the bright side. Instead, I created a series of small successes upon which Adam could build a new attitude. I gave him easy-to-complete assignments, such as inviting a friend over to play video games. As he had more positive contact with his peers, he began to feel more liked by them. We built up his confidence in his ability to play baseball by having him practice in a batting cage. His confidence in his school abilities was improved by having a private tutor work with him to make his skills more automatic and stronger.

A depressed child often lacks both the energy and the confidence to deal with the demands placed upon him. These feelings of helplessness and ineffectiveness can affect a child's schoolwork, social life, and home situation. Defenseless against life's stresses, with little patience to deal with the expectations of teachers, parents, or siblings, a depressed child tends to become rigid in his approaches to everyday life situations. He is inflexible in problem solving and often rejects advice for alternative means of accomplishing a given task. He's put himself in a box from which he doesn't see a way out, and when parents suggest a possible means of escape, he's sure that nothing will work.

A depressed child is likely to be suffering from what well-known psychologist Martin Seligman refers to as learned helplessness. Seligman did a research study on rats in which the rodents received an electric shock no matter where they went in their cages. When he later provided a safe area where the rats could go to avoid the shock, they never used it. They had given up on the idea that the pain could be avoided, and so they didn't even try. Learned helplessness may also apply to the depressed child. She has tried to change her negative situation, but all her efforts have failed. She no longer has any hope that things will get better.

One of my main goals in counseling is to change these feelings and give a child and his family renewed hope that things can get better. Without this hope, it's hard for a child and his family to summon the effort needed to fight and defeat the depression. Why bother working hard at something if you feel that you can't accomplish anything? When a child—and his parent—has hope, the situation has a much greater chance of getting better. Strategies for banishing feelings of helplessness and building confidence will be discussed in more detail in Chapter 10.

Negative Thoughts and Perceptions. Francine sat alone during lunch at school because she felt that the other children didn't like her. She kept to herself because she was afraid that they wouldn't let her join them if she asked to play. Even worse, they might make fun of her if they did. So instead of asking if she could participate in their games, which she really wanted to do, Francine waited for other children to invite her into their circle. Unfortunately, the invitations never came.

Depression impacts not only how a child behaves but also how she thinks about and interprets social situations. It's a familiar story: when you expect the worst, that's exactly what you get. You've created a self-fulfilling prophecy, demonstrating how powerfully our beliefs shape our actions. If you're convinced that other people don't like you, you may treat them coldly or suspiciously or simply avoid them. A child who expects to be disliked by her peers won't be motivated to take the initiative in making social contact with them.

But if she believes that other children will want to play with her and spend time in her company, she'll be more willing to seek them out because she assumes she'll get a positive response from them. Even if a friend says that he has other plans, she may not take it personally, since she's started from the assumption that he likes her. When a child feels unlikable, the risk of having her fears confirmed may make her afraid to ask another child to play.

One of the goals of counseling a depressed child is to replace negative thoughts and expectations with more positive ones. Positive expectations, too, can create self-fulfilling prophecies, this time ones that are more likely to bring about positive results. The tricky part, however, comes in effecting that change. A more complete discussion of how parents can help manage the shift from negative to positive thoughts and perceptions will be addressed in Chapter 13.

Levels of Depression

According to the American Psychiatric Association's *Diagnostic and Statistical Manual of Mental Disorders*, 4th Edition, levels of depression are differentiated by the length and severity of symptoms. Three categories are typically used by psychologists to diagnose depression: major depression, dysthymia, and adjustment disorder with depressed mood. These labels more or less refer to very serious depression, moderate depression, and mild depression, respectively. A child who is totally withdrawn and looks sad all the time may be experiencing a major depression. This type of severe depression might even lead to a child being hospitalized because of her inability to function adequately in everyday circumstances. A child may exhibit a less intense form of depression, such as a depressed mood, or dysthymia, in which the symptoms aren't as strong but they last for a year or more. Adjustment disorder with depressed mood is an even milder form of depression, in which the problem has been noticeable for less than six months and tends to primarily be a response to external stress.

While these labels may be useful in describing the severity of a depression, I don't find them particularly helpful, since my focus is on each individual child and her symptoms and not on a label. Not every child has the same type of negative mood; not every child experiences feelings of sadness or hopelessness in the same way. Focusing on the unique feelings of a child is much more helpful than trying to put her feelings into a category.

Depression Versus Ordinary Sadness

Daniel was fifteen years old and upset because he got cut from his high school basketball team. The coach had called him into his office and told him that he just wasn't fast enough and he could try again another time. Daniel loved basketball, and when he learned that he didn't make the team, he was devastated. He went home and just sat in his room and listened to music for most of the evening. He didn't eat dinner and wouldn't talk to his parents about his tryout. The next morning, he told them what had happened and kept saying how he "sucked" at basketball and would never play again. Eventually, as he shared his feelings with his parents, he began to feel better. By the end of the next day, he was his old self again. While his self-image as a basketball player had taken a hit, he didn't fall into a depression over not making the basketball team.

Feelings of sadness, stress, fatigue, and disappointment are normal, and all of us have experienced them. If that's the case, then what makes these feelings different from the feelings of a child suffering from depression?

- **Depression is persistent over a long period of time.** When the typical child feels sad or unhappy, he can usually work things out in a short time in order to feel better. Depression is more than a one-day event. A child experiencing normal emotions may get very angry or become very sad but will cheer up in a few hours or wake up the next day feeling better. Of course, certain life experiences—the loss of someone close or other traumatic events—may cause deeply felt feelings of sadness in children, and these feelings may persist until a child receives help in dealing with them. However, the depressed child may remain upset or sad for weeks, months, or even years with no apparent traumatic provocation.
- **Depression is more intense than ordinary sadness.** The depressed child simply cannot overcome his intense feelings, and to make matters worse, he can't get his mind off the things that are bothering him. The depressed child is locked into a constant negative cycle. His periods of happiness and well-being are few compared to the times he feels overwhelmed and defeated.

- **Depression is present in all settings.** A child who is depressed experiences sadness, irritability, lack of energy, and hopelessness at home. And in school. And while shopping, playing sports, attending religious services, and visiting family members. There may be momentary relief in some circumstances, but the depression is not experienced in only one place.

Feelings of depression, then, are different from ordinary sadness in many ways. They are more intense, they last longer, and they are evident in school and with peers, as well as at home. A depressed child's eating, sleeping, and playing routines are disturbed, and her self-esteem is at a low ebb. Parents may be aware that a child's facial expressions are different, more rigid and less expressive of ordinary changes in emotion. When healthy children respond to happy events, their smiles and animated facial expressions contrast greatly to the flat or blank affect that depressed children exhibit regardless of circumstances.

One way to get a handle on whether a child is experiencing ordinary sadness or is suffering from depression is to rate her feelings in terms of the following:

- How intense the symptoms are: extreme, moderate, mild
- How long the symptoms last: hours, days, weeks, months
- How pervasive the problems are: at home, at school, with friends

Extreme symptoms that last for weeks or months and are exhibited over a wide range of situations are likely to indicate depression.

Armed with a better understanding of what depression is and how to recognize its signs in children of all ages, parents are better able to decide what to do next for their child. Children suffering from depression *can* be helped. And parents can get the support and guidance they need to help a child step out from under the burden of depression by working with a mental health professional and with a good, well-informed pediatrician.

A Plan for Parents

▶ Don't keep suspicions that your child might be depressed to yourself. Share them with your spouse, pediatrician or family physician, and, most important, your child.

▶ Pick a quiet, relaxed time and place, free of distractions and possible interruptions, and gently and without making any accusations or assumptions, ask your child if something is bothering her. And then listen carefully, asking questions that encourage your child to talk. "Can you tell me more about that?" or "What happened next?" are examples of such questions. Assure your child that she can come to you at any time to talk and that you'll really listen. While this doesn't guarantee that your child will share her problems with you, at least you've opened the door to good communication.

▶ Make sure you have a good pediatrician or family physician with whom you can share your concerns regarding your child's feelings. These doctors are valuable allies in protecting your child's mental and emotional well-being, as well as his physical health.

▶ Try to imagine what your child is feeling, and test out your perceptions by sharing this information with her. While you may assume you know how your child is feeling, you won't know for sure without talking to her. One way for you to approach your child is to share a personal experience with sadness from your own life. You might describe the situation and tell the story of how you were able to deal effectively with difficult feelings. You might also discuss a situation regarding a child you and your child know or even bring up a tele-

vision program, a movie, or a book that can be the
starting point for allowing a child to talk.

► Keep reading and searching the Internet for information
  on depression. Be careful, though, of self-proclaimed
  experts who don't have the credentials or the experience
  to give advice about the subject. Don't assume that
  everything you read on a message board or in a chat
  room is accurate. Instead, look for websites sponsored by
  the National Institute of Mental Health (nimh.nih.gov),
  American Psychological Association (apa.org), National
  Alliance for the Mentally Ill (nami.org), National
  Association of School Psychologists (nasponline.org), or
  American Psychiatric Association (psych.org).

► When choosing books, look for an author who tries to
  give a balanced point of view. Writers who take
  extreme positions may not be practical enough to give
  you guidance for your child's everyday problems. Use
  common sense to help you determine what's relevant
  and what's not. If in doubt, check with your child's
  physician or a mental health professional.

► Never lose hope. Things can get better. I know,
  because I've seen it happen hundreds of times.

2

Diagnosing Childhood Depression

IN ORDER TO make a good and accurate diagnosis, a mental health professional needs good, accurate, and complete information. The assessment process includes meeting with the child, his parents, and even his siblings; finding out about his medical, educational, social, and developmental history; and using instruments developed to help determine how a child is functioning in particular areas of his life. When all these elements are put together, the professional can help a family decide the best course of action to help a child achieve a better, happier life.

How Depression Is Diagnosed in a Child

When your child runs a fever, has a cough, or complains of stomach pains or a sore throat, you can see easily that she's ill. You take her to the doctor, and the doctor monitors her temperature and blood pressure, examines her throat, and perhaps takes a culture sample for further testing. Finally, a diagnosis is made and a course of treatment is prescribed. If your child is suffering from depression, the signs may be harder to spot and more difficult to describe, and the diagnosis and treatment even less familiar.

For generations, parents have been taught about the warning signs of physical illnesses and what to do about them. It's my goal now to help parents acquire the same awareness of depression and the knowledge of how to understand the signs that a child may need help so that proper treatment can be undertaken. Children—and adults!—do best under conditions in which both their physical health and their mental health are properly nurtured.

Consulting a professional, whether a physician or a psychologist, is the best way to get a reliable diagnosis and devise a treatment plan. An experienced clinician will gather information through observing behavior, developing a family history, administering one or more self-reporting rating scales, and conducting a diagnostic interview.

Becoming Your Child's Advocate

Being the parent of a child who's going through a difficult emotional time can feel overwhelming, but let me assure you that you don't need to know all the answers. You are, however, your child's first and best advocate, and therefore you need to know the questions to ask and how to interpret the answers you receive from the professionals you turn to for help. Your concern and your everyday contact with your child are valuable assets in making sure that your child receives the help needed.

Although schools are part of your child's everyday life, you shouldn't count on your child's school to inform you that your child is depressed. Because depressed children may not exhibit overt behavioral or learning difficulties, they are less likely to be referred by teachers to a school psychologist than students who act out, who can't sit still, or who do poorly on tests.

Bear in mind that it takes many steps to diagnose depression. Not only is a single incident an unreliable source of information, but judgments based on a one-time event may keep a child from getting the help she really needs.

▶ **Was Sara Really Depressed?**

Five-year-old Sara, a normally active and energetic child, was admonished at her day care program for hitting another child. In response, Sara shouted out that she wanted to be dead. Her day care teacher then called Sara's mother, Lisa, to say that she had diagnosed Sara as being depressed. The teacher mentioned that she had taken a psychology class at her community college and that Sara fit the profile of a depressed and suicidal child.

Lisa and her husband, Alex, were understandably upset, but they were also a bit confused. They saw Sara as a happy child, always smiling and laughing, who had many friends and enjoyed a variety of activities. In a meeting with Lisa and Alex, the director of the day care program was quite firm in stating that Sara needed to be evaluated by a psychologist. Both he and the teacher, he said, were very worried about her.

Sara's parents didn't agree with his conclusion, but to be safe, they agreed to follow up. They knew Sara had a temper, but they didn't feel that she was depressed. For Alex and Lisa, that single incident didn't constitute a pattern that added up to a diagnosis of depression.

When Sara's parents consulted with me about Sara's emotional state, I spoke to them and then to Sara. I saw an animated little girl who gave no indication that she was unhappy and who had no plan to hurt herself. But Sara—who, like many young children, had trouble expressing some of her complex feelings—did say that she was afraid of being punished by her parents for hitting another child in school. She acknowledged that the worst thing they might do would be to send her to bed early one night and make sure she apologized to the child she had hit. As a result of my interviews and after administering a depression inventory, I concluded that Sara was not suffering from depression.

One statement made in anger by a child may not be reflective of depression or suicidal thinking. Sometimes a child's heightened sense of anxiety or fear is what's really behind an outburst that worries a parent or teacher. Young children often see things in black and white without being aware of the shades of gray and at times may have difficulty saying what they mean. Sara might have said, "I'm afraid of being punished, and I'm upset that everyone is angry with me right now." But most five-year-olds aren't quite so articulate, especially in a moment of stress.

Sara was resilient and not a chronically unhappy or sad child—she was simply a child who had experienced an intensely unhappy moment. A diagnosis of depression is based on many factors that have existed over a period of time. An intense negative reaction on one particular day isn't enough to say that a child is depressed. A young child may make a comment like "I want to die" when he's been punished for doing something wrong. While a child in this situation may feel upset and sad, that moment will pass. Adults, including teachers, may confuse these comments with a serious depression or suicidal behavior.

The Criteria for Diagnosing Depression

In order for a diagnosis of depression to be reached, the following factors (which will be discussed in greater details later in this chapter) must be present:

- An impairment must exist.
- The impairment must be severe enough to interfere frequently with a child's functioning.
- The impairment must have been present for a period of time.
- The impairment must exist across different settings.

So, what's a thoughtful, responsible, concerned parent to do if he believes that his child is exhibiting the signs of depression, as outlined in the previous chapter?

In order to confirm a diagnosis of depression, the first step is to make an appointment with a qualified therapist or physician. (In the next chapter, I'll discuss finding and working with competent people who can help you and your child.) But you can't simply go to a physician's office and tell her to figure out what is wrong with your child. The professional will need to be provided with specific information regarding the nature of the difficulties your child is experiencing. As your child's advocate, you should be aware of what constitutes a good assessment and how you and your family can best prepare for these sessions.

Tools for Assessing Depression

A good assessment takes place when an experienced clinician has considered all possible physical, environmental, or psychological factors that might be causing a change in a child's behavior. Common tools for the assessment of depression are a structured initial interview with the parents and the child and the use of depression scales, such as the Beck Depression Inventory or the Child Depression Inventory.

In a structured interview, parents and children will be asked questions to help the psychologist gather information about the child's health history and his behavior at home, in school, and in interactions with other children and adults. A family history will also be taken.

Of course, the best results come from interviews in which parents and child are as honest and as thorough as possible. The only thing gained from not being completely truthful during assessment interviews is a delay in the process of a child getting better.

This is a time when modesty, embarrassment, or guilt should be left at the door. The goal is to understand the child's behavior, and the only way for a mental health professional to do that properly is to have adequate information. Incomplete or rose-colored information might lead to an incorrect diagnosis or, at the very least, cause the assessment process to become more complicated and longer. For the most part, people *are* honest about their situation and their concerns.

Meeting with the whole family gives the mental health professional so much more information, making it possible to put the pieces together to get the best idea of how the child is functioning. I often find it helpful to involve a child's siblings in the process at some point. A sibling may provide insights that prove useful in the counseling process. As an added benefit, counseling may be helpful for the sibling as well, since she is also impacted by the stress at home.

While some children may initially resist discussing personal issues, if they're truly depressed, they'll want to get help. I can't say this often enough: children do not want to be unhappy and sad. Even children who don't believe that things can ever get better can be encouraged by a psychologist who has the experience and the tools to help the child and his family gain the faith that things can improve.

You should also expect to be asked questions regarding the family history of depression and other mental health issues. A strong family history of depression is a clear signal to me to be aggressive at treating symptoms of depression. Another component of the structured interview will be a review of the child's physical health. Instead of depression, the child might be experiencing significant fatigue and a lack of energy caused by a physical illness or a reaction to medication.

During the initial assessment, suicidal ideation should be explored for any child exhibiting symptoms of depression. Time and again, psychologists have found that talking about depression won't give a child any ideas or increase the risk of suicide. Talking about suicide will, in fact, lessen the probability of a child hurting herself. If you believe that your child may be suicidal, the section at the end of this chapter will provide some suggestions to help you confront this very serious situation.

Preparing for the Initial Interview

In order to prepare for a first meeting with a therapist, parents will find it helpful to write out descriptive narratives that may give the therapist a complete picture of the child and the family situation. If you are prepared with a written summary and have it handy, you are likely to lessen your own anxiety and greatly increase your chance to help your child.

Define Your Child's Problem with Specific Statements. If a parent is unfocused or vague when describing his child's situation, the child may not get the help she needs. Although your child will also be encouraged to tell the doctor what she's experiencing and how long she's felt that way—after all, she is the only one who truly knows what she's feeling—your description of your child's problem is a valuable component in understanding her.

The best descriptions of problems, therefore, are the most specific. For example, a parent might say:

- My daughter misses the school bus about three times a week.
- My son slams doors and throws things when we have arguments.
- My daughter does not get to sleep until two in the morning.

- My son sleeps fourteen hours a day.
- My daughter doesn't talk to us anymore.
- My son is always crying and never seems to smile.
- My daughter tells us she wants to be dead.
- My son has stopped doing his homework and is failing in school.
- My daughter has become more irritable and constantly yells at us.
- My son doesn't listen to me, and taking things away from him has no effect.

Even if the problems you list seem unimportant to you, they'll help a mental health professional see the whole picture. Sometimes, too, the accumulation of apparently little things adds up to a very significant burden for a child.

Describe the History of the Problems. It will be helpful for you to try to determine what factors (internal or external) might be impacting your child's ability to function effectively. One of the best ways to come up with this hypothesis is to conduct a thoughtful review of your child's and your family's prior history, to see if you can identify any specific events that may have triggered or exacerbated the symptoms of depression. Keep in mind that sometimes there is no clear environmental trigger for a child's depression.

On the other hand, what might be perceived as a minor event to you may be a mountain of weight for your child, so even though you may not think an event is important, if something out of the ordinary happened shortly before you noticed a change in your child's behavior, be sure to make a note of it. And while you may not be able to put your finger on the exact trigger for your child's depression, you may be able to identify events that make it worse.

The goal here is to help the mental health professional develop a working hypothesis to guide your child's treatment. No diagnosis in the field of mental health can have the certainty of a medical diagnosis that involves an MRI or a CT scan (and even with those tools, a medical diagnosis may be uncertain). However, parents can help ensure that a competent psychologist will reach a correct diagnosis by providing adequate, accurate, and specific information about the history of the problems and how they currently affect your child.

Prepare a Family History, a School History, and a Health History. Since we've seen that a tendency to depression may be inherited, it's helpful to consider whether any members of the family have ever experienced mental health problems. If they have, it's beneficial to gather information about any medications that might have been used and how the family members responded to treatment.

Your child's school history is an important component of the whole picture of his life. If there's been a change in grades, behavior, or social interactions in school, the interviewer will want to know about that.

As you'll see a little later, some illnesses and even some medications may play a role in changes in a child's behavior, so a health history is another important component of the initial interview.

Possible Components of a Psychological Assessment

Each mental health professional has developed a procedure for conducting an initial structured interview. The initial interview should help a therapist understand what is happening in the child's world, both the interior one and the exterior one, and will serve as the basis for helping parents and children work together to create positive change. Like so many other things, individual styles and experiences vary. But in order to ensure a thorough exploration of a child's situation, several elements should be part of such an interview.

Observation of Body Language, Facial Expression, and Behavior. When a psychologist interviews your child, she is assessing not only what your child is saying but also your child's body language and facial expression. I find that depressed children often exhibit a blank affect, in which they exhibit few facial expressions and rarely smile. A depressed child may walk slowly with his head down and his shoulders slumped. Even his body is signaling that he's depressed. The psychologist will also note how the child interacts with her, how he expresses himself, and how he responds to the environment.

Information About Impairments. Any diagnosis of a disability involves noting impairment in functioning. If a child is meeting the goals that he, his parents, and his teachers have set, it's unlikely that the child is depressed. Once the specific impairments have been described, the psychologist, the child, and the parents will formulate and work toward a series of goals during counseling that relate to those expectations, including peer relationships, school performance, family relationships, self-esteem, concentration, energy level, sleep, thoughts, or general mood.

Degree of Impairment: Is your child so impaired that finishing simple tasks seems as difficult as moving a mountain of sand with a teaspoon? Or is the difficulty less severe, more like moving a mound of sand with a shovel? It's important to try to assess how severely your child's functioning is impacted. Some questions that might help you get a handle on the degree of impairment your child is experiencing include:

- Has there been a recent decline in her work effort or performance?
- Does he experience intense or frequent emotional outbursts?
- Is she neglecting to do chores she once did?
- Are you having more conflict with your child?
- Are your other children having more conflict with him?
- Does she seem more tired and lacking in energy?
- Does he seem to be less happy and talkative than usual?
- Does she avoid doing things that she used to enjoy?

Frequency of Occurrence: How often does your child experience symptoms of impairment? It may be useful to chart how frequently specific problems occur. Consider these questions, for example:

- How many days a week does your child fail to complete chores?
- How many days a week do you have intense arguments with her?

- How often does he talk to you?
- How often do you see her smile?
- How often does he yell at you?
- How often does she get a good night's sleep?

Pervasiveness Across Settings: When a child is depressed, a decline in functioning generally occurs in most settings. While she may still maintain her social life, she may experience more problems than she used to. See if you can pinpoint whether there's a place in which most of the problems occur. Once you are armed with this information, the child, the parent, and the therapist can focus on those areas that need the most attention. You might answer these questions:

- Where does your child exhibit problems?
- Do the problems surface mostly at home?
- Does he experience a lot of problems at school?
- Does she have problems in church, synagogue, or other places of worship?
- Are most of his problems experienced with peers?
- Does she have problems with siblings or other family members?
- With whom are his problems most noticeable?

Review of Family History. A psychologist cannot make a good and accurate diagnosis and treatment plan without conducting a family history. The psychologist needs to be aware of previous emotional traumas, as well as the history of mental health difficulties in the family, since families with a strong history of depression tend to produce children who are at risk for experiencing its symptoms. Of course, that's not the only factor, and a child may be depressed even without a family history that includes depression.

Review of Personal History. Another red flag is significant emotional loss or trauma—these make a child more susceptible to depression. While not every child who experiences a major loss or trauma becomes depressed, these incidents are an important part of the full picture of your child's life. A psychologist needs to know when the symptoms started in order to determine if they are typical of depression or some other problem. The psychologist will also want to determine which events seem to cause the child stress and which ones don't.

Review of Health History. Sometimes a child's symptoms of depression can be a function of a medical condition or a negative reaction to a medication she's taking. Several adolescents I've seen in my practice appeared to have strong symptoms of depression but were actually suffering from mononucleosis. They told me that they were constantly tired and didn't feel like doing anything. They were failing in school and experiencing low self-esteem. When a child exhibits extreme fatigue, it's important to explore medical conditions that might be the source of that reaction. I'd hate to treat a child for depression when, in fact, she had another medical condition. Not only would the child not feel better, but the child's medical and physical health needs would continue to go untreated. That's one important reason why a physician should do a physical exam on any child being evaluated for depression.

A child taking medication for other conditions, such as attention deficit/hyperactivity disorder (ADHD), may experience side effects (for example, irritability and fatigue) that look like depression. But if the symptoms began at the same time the medicine was introduced, they might be side effects of the medication.

Review of School History. A review of your child's school performance can be done by looking at his report card history. If you don't have a copy of your child's report cards, you can get them from your child's school. You have the legal right to a copy of all the information in your child's school folder. A review of your child's school history will tell you if there are problems at school and when they started. Getting this information can be critical in making an accurate diagnosis of depression.

Review of Peer Relationships. If your child has cut himself off from other children, this may be a sign of depression. Also, depressed children have a way of finding each other. If most of your child's friends appear to be unhappy and have suffered from depression, this might be a sign that your child is also depressed.

Review of Work Products. Samples of your child's artwork and writing may be useful in assessing her for depression. Children express many of their feelings in artwork and writing, and if your child is depressed, a dark and hopeless quality will probably permeate her drawings, stories, and essays.

Review of Music Taste. An obsession with music dealing with death, dying, or sadness could indicate a depressed mood. It would be most alarming if this were the only type of music your child listens to. If your child has a wide range of musical tastes, then the occasional darker-toned CD wouldn't be a cause for major concern.

Assessment for Other Mental Health Conditions. Because children with depression often suffer from other conditions (such as ADHD, anxiety, or obsessive-compulsive disorder) or may be involved in substance abuse, it's important that an initial assessment considers these conditions. (These conditions will be discussed in greater detail in Chapter 6.)

Your child is less likely to get better if you focus on only one part of her problem and ignore others. If she has a significant substance abuse problem, it will be difficult to treat the depression without also treating the substance abuse. Proper and effective treatment, therefore, depends on a full assessment to determine whether other mental health issues need to be addressed in order to help a child move toward a happier, more productive future.

Before a child is diagnosed with depression, other mental health conditions must be ruled out through a process called differential diagnosis. Many depressed children have problems paying attention and completing their schoolwork—but so do children with other problems. One factor that distinguishes depression from other mental health conditions, such as ADHD, is the onset of the problems. A child with ADHD will always have had difficulties paying attention, and those problems are likely to have been noted in a child's school records. With depression, on the other hand, a child's problems are more apt to be relatively recent in origin.

Administration of a Depression Scale

As part of the assessment, a psychologist may administer a depression scale, a test that has been standardized to give mental health professionals a clearer idea of the extent of a child's depression.

Psychologists may use one of the many good depression scales, such as Achenbach, Connors, or BASC. My personal preference for assessing depression is to use the Child Depression Inventory (designed for ages seven to seventeen) for preadolescents and the Beck Depression Inventory-II (designed for ages thirteen to eighty) for older adolescents. I've also used the Beck Youth Inventory for middle school–aged children.

These scales focus specifically on depression, asking questions about the child's energy level, sleep patterns, concentration, self-esteem, irritability, and thoughts of self-harm. The tests usually take about ten minutes to complete, during which time a child who can read fills out a questionnaire. A psychologist usually spends another ten to twenty minutes reviewing the answers with the child. If a child can't read, then the questions should be read to him. In my years of practice, I've found the depression scales that I've used to be accurate reflectors of a child's feelings.

Depending on the score your child receives after answering the questions, the depression scale may indicate that your child has no symptoms, mild symptoms, moderate symptoms, or severe symptoms of depression.

Personal Interview Based on Answers to Depression Scale. A child's responses to a rating scale are often the best opening for me to start asking questions, since trying to clarify a child's meaning is a natural outcome of the testing process. For example, when Roberta, a nine-year-old whose parents were worried because she spent a lot of time alone in her room, reported that she was often sad and cried a lot, this provided me with an opening to ask her about her feelings. Roberta thought for a while and then slowly started talking about how she was unhappy because her parents had moved to a new neighborhood and she missed her best friend, who used to live next door. She went on to say that she hadn't made any new friends and felt left out at her new school. Armed with this knowledge, I was eventually able to help Roberta take steps to deal more effectively with the lack of contact with her friend and learn new ways to make friends at school.

Depression and the Risk of Suicide

Three million teenagers consider or attempt suicide
    every year.
Suicide is the third leading cause of death in adolescents.
Approximately one-fourth of adolescent deaths are
    the result of suicide.
While girls are more likely to make attempts, boys are
    more likely to complete the act.

Do I have your attention? Good, because this is serious business. Even if it doesn't seem to apply to your child at this time, please read this section carefully. You may be able to assist another parent help a child at risk. Suicide is hard to talk about and hard to think about, but please don't skip this section. Adults who are well informed are a child's best ally in times of crisis.

How can you determine whether your child is at risk to commit suicide?

For parents, this is a difficult question to consider. It's much easier to say, "Oh, that's not something that applies to my child, so I don't even want to think about it." But I urge you to do just that.

If you remember your own childhood and adolescence, you probably can recall times when you were sad, angry, disappointed. Maybe some of your behavior was an attempt to test the adults in your life—teen music and dress have long been arenas where a little rebellion has been expressed—and you wonder whether your child's behavior is part of a normal developmental process or a sign that something is seriously wrong.

Unfortunately, no book can give you a definitive answer. What I can do is give you a sense of some of the indicators that have been linked to children who are at risk. In a family with a history of suicidal behavior, these signs may be even more significant, because while most children with severe depression do not commit suicide, these children are at significantly higher risk for making a suicide attempt.

If your child has experienced a significant loss, such as the death of a parent or another loved one, a breakup with a girlfriend or boyfriend, academic failure, sexual abuse, a move to a new town, or the suicide of a friend or family member, he may be at greater risk. When drug or alcohol abuse is added to the mix, the risk increases further.

Although parents may have no idea about a child's emerging sexuality, it's important to be aware that gay and lesbian teenagers are at significantly greater risk for suicide. Sadly, the enormous pressures placed on these children by society may create a sense of despair that leads to feelings of utter hopelessness. A child who self-identifies as a gay or lesbian teen is a child likely to be more prone to depression and to be at greater risk for committing suicide.

A parent's job is complicated by the fact that the problems that are most troubling to a child may be the hardest for him to talk about. Even when there's good communication between parents and children, teens especially may keep the most troublesome aspects of their lives to themselves.

Questions to Answer If You Think Your Child May Be Considering Suicide

- Has your child shown a dramatic improvement without having received treatment, such as counseling or medication? When a child is severely depressed, he may not have enough energy to plan and carry out an attempt to kill himself. But sometimes when a severely depressed child starts to feel a little better, the risk for harming himself may increase. A child recovering from a major depression may need extra monitoring. This may be especially true when the child suffers a minor relapse during the initial recovery period. Sometimes suicidal children get a burst of energy when they finalize the decision to kill themselves.

- Has your depressed child given away important or favorite possessions to friends? Such activities may indicate that a child wants to make sure that someone will care for the possessions and, in a very sad way, care for him.

- Has your child exhibited recent self-abusive behavior, such as cutting or hitting herself or making extremely derogatory remarks about herself?

- Does your child listen constantly to dark music that refers to death and suicide or write poems, stories, or essays about death and suicide?

- Have you seen a dramatic increase in your child's risk-taking behavior? If a child has suddenly started driving too fast and too recklessly, walking inappropriately into heavy traffic, walking dangerously near active railroad tracks, or using excessive amounts of dangerous drugs, he may be sending a signal about wanting to end his life.

- Has your child made comments about wanting to be dead or about committing suicide? If your child does make suicidal comments, you must take them very seriously. As I said earlier, talking about suicide has not been shown to give children ideas where none existed. Instead, such conversations can be the starting point in assuring that a child gets the help he needs.

What to Do If You Believe Your Child Is at Risk for Committing Suicide

If you answered yes to any of these questions, you should make contact with a mental health professional to have your child assessed for both depression and suicide risk.

- **First, talk to your child.** Pick a quiet time, with no distractions and with no one else around, so that you can let your child know that your focus is on him alone and that you're treating him with respect and concern. During your discussion, ask your child whether he has a plan to commit suicide. If he does, ask him if he has a time and place in mind for making the attempt.

- **Remove all firearms from the home.** Be aware that guns and rifles have been increasingly used, especially by boys, in committing suicide. If you believe your child is suicidal, it is imperative to make sure that he has no access to firearms. It's not enough to hide guns and rifles in the back of a closet. With your child's safety at stake, it's far more prudent not to have any firearms in the home.
- **Contact a professional.** If you believe your child is at risk for committing suicide, you should contact your child's pediatrician to get a referral to a mental health provider or mental health clinic.

  If your child cannot be seen that day, get the name of a local hospital that does suicide risk assessments. Many hospital emergency rooms have this service. However, not all hospitals are equal. Ideally, your child should be assessed at a psychiatric hospital that specializes in the treatment of children and adolescents. Even if you have to travel to get to one, the minor inconvenience is worth the effort in protecting your child. Sitting around in a waiting room with very disturbed adults may make your child feel that she is "really crazy." This may make her less likely to cooperate with the treatment.

  Schools may be equipped to give advice on treatment options. A call to a guidance counselor, school social worker, or school psychologist may also be helpful.

  Crisis centers, open twenty-four hours a day, 365 days a year, serve many communities. Through these services, you will be directed to help for your child. You can call 800-SUICIDE (800-784-2433) or go online to hopeline.com to find a crisis center in your area.

- **Have a crisis plan ready.** Although you may want to get immediate help for your child, there are times when the medical system may not be as responsive as you'd like. Hospitals are often short-staffed around holidays. You may live far from a good facility. For whatever reasons, it may take hours or even days before your child receives help.

While you're waiting for help, you should put into action a crisis plan that will be helpful in keeping your child safe and in keeping you alert and aware of her condition.

A good crisis plan should include being in constant close proximity to your child until the crisis is over. To help pass the time, distractions such as music or video games may be valuable. Maybe you and your child have enjoyed activities in the past, such as playing cards or going for a walk, which you can do together. You might encourage your child to use relaxation techniques, such as deep breathing and positive imagery, to help calm her.

And don't forget to take care of yourself. A series of slow, deep breaths and the positive image of helping your child through the crisis may help keep you focused on the true task, which is to keep your child safe and get him the help he needs. Inviting a caring friend or relative to visit with you to assist in the crisis might provide the support you need to maintain a calm and steady presence.

A Plan for Parents

► Make a list of the things that concern you regarding your child's difficulties. Then divide these difficulties into two lists: those that you can address later on and those that need your immediate attention.

► Ask for help whenever you feel your child is at any risk for hurting herself. This is not a problem you should handle by yourself. It's better to err on the side of being too cautious than to take a chance with your child's life.

► Be conservative and schedule an appointment with a mental health professional, even if you are not sure your child is depressed.

▼

PART II

Charting a Course

Treating Childhood Depression

- ▶ Who should be treating my child?
- ▶ How can I find a competent therapist?
- ▶ What can I expect to happen during therapy?
- ▶ What kinds of therapy might apply to my child?
- ▶ When is medication included in treatment?
- ▶ What medications might be used, and in what doses?
- ▶ Will medication increase the risk of suicide in my child?
- ▶ How can I tell if my child is experiencing adverse side effects of medication?
- ▶ What other mental health issues might coexist with depression, and how do they affect treatment?
- ▶ What if I suspect my child has bipolar disorder?
- ▶ Why are some children hospitalized or placed in residential treatment?

3

Working with a
Mental Health Professional

▶ Mr. and Mrs. Rutherford, very private people, were reluctant to take their son Charles for counseling because they didn't want to share intimate details of their family life with a complete stranger they weren't sure they could trust.

In their hearts, they knew something was wrong with Charles. He had nightmares, his teacher had called several times to say that he'd gotten into fights, and he'd stopped going to Little League practice. Whenever they tried to talk to him about what he was feeling, Charles answered that he just didn't care about anything and then went off to his room as soon as he could get away.

The Rutherfords tried to give him rewards for participating in baseball, they left the light on in the hall at night, and they tried to talk to him about ways to resolve differences without fighting. But nothing changed. Although they sensed, as many parents do, that their child wasn't behaving like himself, they tried to convince themselves that Charles was going through a passing phase that would go away on its own.

This may be true some of the time, but too many problems don't simply evaporate.

How much better it would be, the Rutherfords finally realized, to go to a psychologist and be told that their child has no problem than to sit on a problem that would continue to get worse without treatment. An infection on a child's knee needs prompt attention so that it can be treated before it requires extreme action. Similarly, the longer an emotional problem exists, the more difficult it can be to treat. The Rutherfords agreed that their son needed more help than they were able to give him. After much thought and discussion, they finally decided that they would give counseling a try because Charles's pediatrician had recommended that they do so, and they trusted her.

Deciding to See a Mental Health Professional

Whenever Mr. and Mrs. Rutherford thought about their upcoming visit with the recommended psychologist, they were filled with apprehension, because they didn't know what to expect. How deeply would the psychologist probe into their personal lives? What if she expressed contempt for parents who couldn't figure out what to do to make things better for their own child? What would she think of their parenting skills? What if she told them that she thought they were the cause of Charles's problems?

If they had understood a little more about what to expect during the sessions with the psychologist, they might have gotten help for their child sooner, and it might have been a more comfortable, less anxiety-provoking situation. Mental health professionals are in the business of helping others. Rather than looking down on parents who bring their child in to be evaluated for depression, they're more likely to have a feeling of respect and honor. They understand that you've gone through a lot before deciding to seek treatment for a child and that you've probably tried to fix the problem on your own, without achieving the results you so wanted. They look forward to sharing their training and experience with you, to help develop new treatment strategies that will allow you and your child to feel better.

A good counselor will provide you with hope that your child's feelings of sadness and impairment will improve. A family needs that hope in order to put forth its best effort to help resolve the problems that made them seek assistance. A therapist will also listen carefully to all the family members and create a climate in which each person feels accepted and valued. Anyone who feels that she is being judged by a therapist is much more likely to experience problems during counseling.

The ideal climate for counseling, then, is one of mutual respect and trust. You should respect the expertise of the therapist and in return feel respected and understood by him. This environment allows families working with a counselor to develop new ways of thinking about problems, strategies for dealing with stressful events, and improved means of communicating with each other. Improvement doesn't happen in a totally predictable way, of course. Every road contains a few bumps. Still, your family should expect concrete results after participating in a few counseling sessions.

Seeking Help Is a Family Decision

After Mr. and Mrs. Rutherford decided to make an appointment with a psychologist, they sat down with Charles and told him that they wanted to go as a family to see if a psychologist could help them make their family situation better.

Actively involving your child in the decision to see a psychologist can help get things off to a good start. You need to be sensitive to the way he feels. Saying that he needs to see a psychologist could be, for him, the equivalent of saying that he's crazy. It's best not to bring up the matter when you're angry or frustrated. Instead, the upcoming visit should be discussed calmly. You can start by saying that you believe that the family has a problem to work on and that it would be helpful to go as a family to a mental health professional. If you make it clear that this is a group process, the child will probably feel better about participating.

Choosing a Professional

Once you've determined that your child should be evaluated for depression, the next question is, how do you find a competent professional to work with your family? For many parents, the first person to turn to will be the child's pediatrician or the family physician. Your child's pediatrician will want to refer you to a person she trusts. If she sends you to someone who isn't competent, her reputation and your relationship with her will be compromised.

You might also contact a friend you trust or someone you know who is already seeing a psychologist. Another referral source is your child's school. Most schools have access to a school nurse, school psychologist, guidance counselor, or school social worker who may be able to help get the ball rolling for you.

When it comes to counseling your child, I highly recommend that you seek the services of either a psychologist or a social worker. Of course, a diploma or a license doesn't guarantee that an individual will be just right for you and your child. As in any other field, it's the quality of the person rather than the degree alone that will determine what kind of service you receive.

But working your way through the maze of degrees, licenses, and certifications can seem like a daunting task, and to make matters even more challenging, states may have different specific requirements, health insurance providers may cover certain kinds of care and not others, and reaching a good mental health professional at the end of that maze might seem impossible. It's not! But you do need to know what some of the language means and how to take those first steps.

Pediatrician

Very often, the primary source for help when a child has problems is her physician. If you trust the pediatrician with your child's physical health, you'll probably trust him with issues related to your child's mental health. Physicians enjoy a high level of trust in our society, and many parents consult with them on problems that appear to be related to mental health.

A pediatrician is a trained medical doctor who specializes in the care of children, although he probably doesn't have specialized training in the area of counseling or psychology. However, pediatricians are often on the front lines for dealing with mental health difficulties, such as ADHD, anxiety, or depression. Even though they didn't spend extra years of training in mental health issues, as psychiatrists do, they've probably developed a lot of expertise through seeing patients over the years. Instead of receiving specialized formal training at a college or hospital, they get on-the-job training.

Many physicians refer a patient to a psychiatrist, psychologist, or social worker when they feel that the source of a child's illness isn't physical. Just as some pediatricians would refer a patient with a mysterious rash to a dermatologist, they may prefer to have your child see a psychiatrist and/or a psychologist to treat mental health issues. In fact, the majority of referrals in my private practice come from physicians. A team effort, in which a psychologist and the family work with a physician, is often very effective in treating a child's depression.

For a physician to adequately treat depression, parents will need to provide periodic feedback regarding their child's progress. Bringing progress reports from your child's school, scheduling periodic visits with your physician, and maintaining good communication between the physician and the psychologist or social worker who is seeing your child are all components of a good treatment plan.

Family Physician

The family physician is a medical doctor trained to view individual patients within the context of the family unit. The patient-physician relationship is developed and nurtured with a knowledge of all medical, behavioral, and emotional aspects of the family and each of its members. This training provides a good starting point for assessing and treating mental health issues such as depression, which may have a genetic component.

Like the pediatrician, family physicians frequently refer children to psychologists and social workers for ongoing counseling and will remain part of the team with whom your child and family will have regular contact.

Child Psychiatrist

A child is typically referred to a psychiatrist if the use of medication is being considered for treating a mental health condition. Most psychiatrists provide assessment and diagnosis and determine what medication(s), if any, would offer the most effective treatment. While some psychiatrists do counseling, most are involved primarily in managing a child's medication regime. This is an important job—the right medication can be extremely helpful and the wrong one very damaging. Chapter 5 will discuss the medication question in greater detail.

While most psychiatrists would prefer to avoid prescribing medication and still have a child make progress toward recovering from depression, they also believe that in some instances medication may be truly useful in helping a child begin the journey toward wellness.

Because the proper knowledge of medication and its potential effects is so important, working with a psychiatrist who has a good reputation among other medical professionals is highly recommended. Your child's pediatrician, family physician, or psychologist would be a good referral source to find the right child psychiatrist and may even be able to help you get an appointment in a doctor's crowded schedule. The current shortage of good child psychiatrists in most areas of the country means that they often have a heavy caseload and appointments may be hard to come by.

A recent survey conducted by the American Medical Association indicated that there are only 7,200 accredited child and adolescent psychiatrists in the United States. If you think about it, this means that with the population under the age of eighteen reaching about seventy-three million in 2000, there was one child psychiatrist for every one hundred thousand children. This is an exceptionally low ratio and pretty much guarantees that some parents won't have access to the services of a child psychiatrist. Typically, child psychiatrists aren't compensated as well as other medical specialists, and they have to spend more time than most physicians returning calls to their patients, so the shortage may not be alleviated anytime soon.

When choosing a child psychiatrist, it's important to find somebody who will return your telephone calls and take your concerns seriously. All medications can have potential side effects, and it's vital that you work with someone you trust will get back to you quickly if you suspect your child has a problem. Any physician, including a psychiatrist, should provide contact information for a backup person to answer questions regarding a child's medication if the physician is on vacation, out for the evening, or otherwise unavailable.

Like a pediatrician, a psychiatrist is a medical doctor who can prescribe medication. However, the difference is that psychiatrists went to medical school and then completed three to four years of specialized training in the field of mental health. Besides having more thorough knowledge of mental health disorders than most pediatricians, they tend to have the most current knowledge of new medications to treat them.

When seeing a child psychiatrist, you can expect to have an initial sixty- to ninety-minute interview. The psychiatrist may administer rating scales and talk to the parents and the child individually. The goal of the psychiatrist is to adequately diagnose the child's condition and determine whether she would benefit from a specific type of medication. The second session will generally be much shorter, often half an hour, and will focus on the child's adjustment to the medication.

Psychiatric Nurse Practitioner

Psychiatric nurse practitioners are a viable alternative to getting medications if you are unable to get an appointment with a child psychiatrist. In many states, a psychiatric nurse practitioner is required to have a master's degree in nursing and is likely to spend another two years getting a certificate degree, which allows him to prescribe psychiatric medications, usually in collaboration with a child psychiatrist. A psychiatric nurse practitioner is eligible for third-party reimbursement from most health insurance companies. Like so many other regulations, the particulars governing training as well as the ability to prescribe medication and to receive insurance reimbursements may vary from state to state, but even if it takes a little extra time to track down all the necessary information, this option may be a good one in situations where it is difficult to see a child psychiatrist.

Licensed Psychologist

Let's clear up the common confusion between the terms *psychologist* and *psychiatrist*. The major difference is that a psychologist is not a medical doctor and therefore cannot prescribe medication. If your child needs medication, he will need to get a prescription from a pediatrician or a child psychiatrist.

A psychologist usually has finished four to five years of graduate study after college, has completed a doctoral dissertation, and has passed a licensing exam. Specialty fields differ. A person can hold a doctorate in clinical psychology, counseling psychology, school psychology, or educational psychology. And the names of the degrees differ, too. A psychologist may have a Ph.D. (doctor of philosophy) or a Psy.D. (doctor of psychology). The Psy.D. is a more practice-oriented degree; the Ph.D. dissertation work tends to be more theoretical. With a Ph.D., the psychologist who wants to teach at a college or do research may be given preference over one with a Psy.D.

A psychologist usually schedules counseling sessions lasting about forty-five minutes. At the start of your family's relationship with a psychologist, you can expect to fill out paperwork (insurance papers, for example) and a release of information so that communication can be shared between your psychologist and your pediatrician. You might also be asked to fill out rating scales or forms regarding your concerns for your child.

Once you get into the psychologist's office, the process of assessing the problem and making a plan for the future will begin. When I first meet with a family, I try to let them know that my job is to help make a difficult situation better. I need to find out what they perceive the problem to be and instill a feeling of optimism in the family. I usually see the family together, as well as the parents alone and the child alone. Before the appointment is over, we all get together to review what happened and develop a plan of action. Some psychologists may have a different procedure, but this one is common practice.

Social Worker

Social workers may have an advantage over psychologists when it comes to training, because family counseling is often a focus of their preparation. They may have a disadvantage in that they may have less training in psychological theory. Social workers often have a two-year postgraduate degree and may have participated in an internship that provides supervised practical experience. A social worker can be as competent as (or more competent than!) a psychologist. So much depends upon the person and how he matches up with your family. Social workers can work in clinics, school settings, or private practice. They are likely to have a master in social work (M.S.W.) degree and are also sometimes called licensed or certified social workers

(C.S.W. or L.C.S.W., respectively). Unlike master's-level psychologists, most social workers are eligible to receive third-party payments from health insurance companies.

Master's-Level Psychologist

Master's-level psychologists usually aren't licensed. They may work in clinics, schools, or state education offices. While they may have good skills, they may not be eligible for certification or licensing because they lack one or more state requirements—and each state does have a different set of requirements. Because they aren't licensed, they are likely to be ineligible for third-party payments, and so your health insurance might not reimburse you for their services.

Psychotherapist

Anyone can call herself a psychotherapist, so parents should be especially careful in dealing with such a practitioner. It's a term that has no formal meaning in evaluating training and experience, and it's therefore difficult to judge whether the psychotherapist might truly help your family. Without the qualifications to do counseling, the psychotherapist may end up prolonging a family's problems, so it's extremely important that you check out the person's background before scheduling an appointment. A degree or expertise in a particular area may be hard to confirm, but it's worth taking the time to check whether the person's background is truly appropriate for working with your child.

Getting Your Child to Go for Counseling

Your child probably wants to be free of the confines of the tight, dark world of depression, but she needs your guidance and encouragement to take those first steps forward toward greater health and happiness. Anytime you can get your child to go with you to visit a mental health professional, you have helped her begin that journey.

Even if your child is resistant and complains but allows herself to be nudged forward by her concerned parent, she is communicating a message. In essence, she's saying, "Some part of me is willing to try this because I want to get better." If a child is in my office, then at least I have an opening. If I need to, I become a salesman. I can accomplish something if only I can get my foot in the door—or, in this case, get the foot of the child in my office.

If a child refuses to come to my office, I often call him on the telephone and explain that he has nothing to be worried about. Anxious children who are afraid of what will happen in the doctor's office are the ones who often refuse to come in, so it's part of my job to help diminish that anxiety. I usually tell the child that he doesn't have to say or do anything in my office and that all I want is his presence. I also tell him my first rule: the child is boss in my office. He can do what he wants, with one exception: nothing and nobody is to get hurt.

Giving a child the feeling that she will have some control over what goes on in my office is one element that helps overcome initial reluctance and anxiety about participating in therapy. I also tell her that I'll ask her parents for permission to keep my conversations with her confidential. The exception to this confidentiality, and I say this to children so that they understand before we begin, concerns talk of a child's having the intention to hurt herself or somebody else. Another obvious exclusion I mention is the allegation of child abuse, for which I am a mandated reporter.

If the child is still uncomfortable with the process, I offer to make a deal for him to come in for three sessions. If he's still uncomfortable with the process after that, he won't have to come back. Very few children have exercised this option on me. Once the child realizes that counseling can be a nonthreatening process and help is being provided to him, he keeps his appointments.

When I encounter a child with a severe substance abuse issue, the process is different. Too many times, a child who gets high regularly is so altered by drugs or alcohol that she feels no motivation to participate in treatment. In the worst of these situations, it's my opinion that inpatient hospitalization to deal with the addiction may be required before significant progress can occur.

If all your efforts to get your child to come in for counseling are still unsuccessful, I urge you to make an appointment for yourself with a mental health professional, to explore strategies that may help you deal with the situation in your family.

Making Your First Appointment

Sometimes that journey you're trying to help your child undertake may stall before it begins because you don't know what to expect. Most mental health professionals welcome questions on the telephone prior to a family's visit. We do what we can to help parents and children feel more comfortable about what they're about to experience. I've been asked questions such as these:

- Can I leave my other children unattended in the waiting room?
- Do I need to bring a copy of my insurance card?
- Should I bring a copy of my child's school records?
- Will I have a chance to talk to you [the therapist] alone?
- How long will the sessions be?
- How confidential will our sessions be?
- Are you [the therapist] available to talk to my child's teachers?
- How often will my child need to have appointments?
- Are evening or weekend appointments available?
- What areas of mental health do you [the therapist] specialize in?
- What is the procedure when I have an emergency situation with my child?

Your therapist should provide honest, complete, and clear answers that help diminish your worries and contribute to the feeling that things really can improve.

Confidentiality

Two kinds of confidentiality apply to counseling involving parents and kids. The first may be difficult for parents to accept, but it's such an essential part of building trust with a child that even though I've mentioned it before, I'll say it again.

I always ask parents to allow their child the freedom to talk confidentially with me and allow me to tell the child that our discussions won't be shared with anyone without her permission. The exceptions—making a plan to hurt herself or indications of child abuse (which most states mandate that mental health professionals, doctors, and educators report)—now also include treatment reports that so many managed care companies require in order to approve of continuing services.

The second kind of confidentiality involves public disclosure. A therapist will not release information regarding the sessions with you, your child, or your family without your permission. Whether it's a school guidance counselor, a curious neighbor, or a newspaper reporter, if anyone asks me a question about a client, my standard response is that I never share information about any of my clients without parental permission.

Paying for Mental Health Services

In the United States, people are forever talking about the health care system and how to make quality care available to everyone. Until something better comes along, we all have to deal with the realities, and some of them require a little creative thinking and a lot of open discussion with your health care providers.

Your health insurance policy will determine how much reimbursement you'll receive for your child's counseling sessions. You may be responsible for a co-pay fee at each session, just as you would with any other doctor. This fee varies and may range from $10 to $50 or more, depending upon your insurance. Many managed care insurance policies have an escalating co-pay fee that goes up after several visits. With a managed care policy, you may also be limited to a specified number of covered visits. Very often, the psychologist or social worker has to write a report to justify additional visits. This can be a time-consuming process that most consumers aren't aware of, but it's one of the realities we providers must live with.

If you don't have health insurance coverage, you can expect to pay anywhere from $100 to $150 for an initial session and an average of $100 to $120 for follow-up sessions. For many families, this expense can be prohibitive, so some psychologists may see you for a lower fee, on a sliding scale, if you make arrangements before the visit. I often work out a payment plan on a sliding scale with parents if a child isn't covered by insurance. Also, your child may be eligible for a supplemental Medicaid program that allows children to get health insurance for little or no money. Each state has its own policy on this type of insurance. You can investigate your child's eligibility for these programs at her pediatrician's office, her school, or your local Department of Social Services.

Currently, treatment for mental health concerns doesn't receive the same level of benefits as physical health treatments with most insurance plans. Many proposals are now before Congress to provide for parity and guarantee full coverage to both adults and children with mental health conditions, such as depression. You may want to write to your representative or senator in support of parity for mental health benefits.

A Plan for Parents

- ► Discuss the decision to go to counseling with your child before the first visit.
- ► Try to obtain health insurance that has good mental health benefits.
- ► Get a referral from someone you trust. Try to avoid using the yellow pages.
- ► If your child is in crisis, contact your pediatrician for referral to a local hospital. Otherwise, take the time necessary to find someone who has a good reputation.
- ► Review the expectations that you have for the counseling process to determine if they are being met by your therapist.
- ► Go to the counseling session with a list of issues or concerns that you'd like to see addressed.
- ► Give the counseling sessions a few visits, and if you aren't comfortable, switch to another counselor.

4

Counseling for Depression

THERE IS NO one-size-fits-all approach for children who are depressed. Counseling strategies should be tailored to the unique needs of your child and your family, as well as to the experiences and abilities of the treating therapist.

Counseling is designed to help your child feel better and be better able to meet the demands of his life situation. Depression is not an isolated event—it impacts all areas of a child's life.

Whenever a child comes to me for counseling, I start by focusing on the impairment the child is experiencing. By doing this, I can identify which symptoms need to be treated. Eventually, this allows me to determine when the child no longer needs counseling. Also, by looking at the impairments, I'm forced to focus on the child, rather than on some label or a theoretical description. Some psychologists or psychiatrists label a patient with a disorder and see the disorder, not the person. But not every child with depression has the same symptoms, nor do they suffer with the same degree of severity.

By keeping the child's impairments central, I'm also keeping my eye on the goals of treatment. Those aspects of the child's life that need to be improved receive my attention. If I were to focus on the depression in general, I might lose sight of the distress the child is experiencing and the specific needs she's developed.

Not treating depression can have serious consequences. It can impair a child's development of social and academic skills and can lead to antisocial behavior, alcohol and substance abuse, and even suicide.

What Happens During Counseling

Some therapists may take a cognitive behavioral approach, some emphasize behavior modification strategies, others focus on family dynamics, and some take a psychoanalytic approach. However, I find that most psychologists use a combination of treatment approaches. While they may prefer one predominant mode of treatment, they use other approaches when appropriate. If a therapist is rigid and focuses on only one type of treatment, he may be less effective with a particular child who may respond better to other forms of therapy. Children come into my office with an astonishing variety of problems, symptoms, and needs—not all depressions are the same. Canned solutions are about as effective as prescribing the same pair of eyeglasses for every nearsighted patient.

No matter what the treatment strategy, the foundation for effective treatment is the establishment of a good working relationship between the therapist and the child and her family. Without that relationship, positive change is unlikely to occur. Actually, the relationship between the family and the therapist tends to be a better predictor of the child's success in counseling than the particular counseling strategy being used.

The comfort factor is a major component of the relationship between therapist, child, and family, one that is the starting point for successful treatment. The precise qualities that make a parent comfortable with one therapist but not with another are surely personal— one might describe it as having good chemistry with a counselor. Many variables play a part in the comfort factor. The first is trust— this person, after all, will be someone with whom you need to be honest and thorough in talking about difficult issues. A therapist's office should be a safe place to talk. Just as I wouldn't allow a fellow to repair my furnace if I didn't trust him, I surely wouldn't want a therapist to "work on" me or my child without trusting that she knew what she was doing.

Another component of the comfort factor is respect—being in counseling with a therapist you don't respect or one who you feel disrespects you is likely to lead to poor results. Your therapist should give you hope that things will be better. She should also leave you with the feeling that you and your child are being listened to and understood without being judged. And you should never feel intimidated by a counselor. Don't be afraid to ask your psychologist questions and clarify issues you want to know more about.

After going to counseling for several weeks, your child should show positive changes and your whole family should feel benefits. The changes might be small or they might be significant, but they should be noticeable. If they're not, you should bring this up with your therapist. If you aren't happy with the reply, it may be time to switch to a new therapist.

Understanding a bit about the most frequently used therapies may help you feel more comfortable in talking to the counselor. Remember: most counselors these days use a combination of approaches to craft the best treatment for each child, family, and problem.

Cognitive Behavioral Therapy

Cognitive behavioral therapy is a common approach that works toward changing the way you think about things. The central idea is that what you think will affect how you feel—the words you use to describe a situation have a big impact on how you feel about that situation. If I get a C on a test that I wanted to ace, I can tell myself I am stupid and will never succeed—or I can tell myself I didn't do too well on this test, so I'll have to put in a little extra effort to make up for it next time. With the first message, I feel defeated before I even start, but with the second, I feel energized to work hard for what I want.

Cognitive behavioral therapy tries to challenge a child's beliefs or thoughts so that she shifts from negative thinking to more positive thoughts. A therapist's goal might be to get a child to question and change the negative ideas and self-talk that have become part of her thinking. A depressed, unhappy person is far more likely to focus

on what's wrong with her life than to spend a lot of time acknowledging its positive aspects. By breaking the cycle, the therapist tries
to prevent negative thinking from leading to more depression and to
encourage more positive thoughts to create a brighter mood.

Children who are depressed also tend to generalize, so that they
see things as all bad instead of being aware of the shades of gray. A
difficult homework assignment, a fight with a girlfriend, and a hole
in a new leather jacket all become equally awful—the most awful, in
fact. Some children may also blame themselves and feel responsible
for events that are really not their fault—the illness of a sibling, for
example, or a strain in the parents' relationship. I also find that
depressed children can be rigid in their way of thinking, which limits what they consider as possible solutions to their problems. They
feel trapped, confined to a box they can't get out of. They usually feel
helpless and lack confidence in their ability to improve their situation.

Cognitive behavioral therapy works to change a child's assumptions and theories to new ones that better serve her. A child whose
parent committed suicide may assume an unreasonable and irrational
blame for the death. She may believe that her mother wouldn't have
died if she had been with her, or she might feel that she could have
done something that would have prevented the suicide. I try to help
the child understand that the death wasn't her fault, by challenging
her assumptions and beliefs. I explain that her mother was mentally
ill and had a sickness that was just as fatal as any cancer could be. I
then try to point out to the child that she isn't a doctor and that she
has no training to treat such an illness. My goal is to help the child
blame the illness instead of herself. Often, several sessions are required
before the child can relinquish her self-blame and come up with a
more logical understanding of her parent's death. Without therapy,
the child may experience a strong and extensive depression as a result
of this self-blame.

The ultimate goal of this kind of therapy is to develop more positive, flexible, and effective ways of thinking. Changing the way a
child describes a situation to herself often allows the way she feels
about it to change. If she perceives that she is no longer trapped in
a box with no way out, she should feel more hopeful about her cur-

Strategies for Developing More Positive Thoughts

- Ask your child to write down one positive thing she did each day.
- Have your child keep a daily log of his thoughts so that you can both track how many negative and positive thoughts he has each day.
- Encourage your child to think about the probability of her negative thoughts being accurate. Questioning the negative thoughts may lead your child to develop more positive ones or at least be more open to them.
- Invite your child to think of multiple solutions to problems. If he fixates on only one possible solution, he'll probably miss others that would be helpful to him.
- Evaluate your own thoughts about your child. If they are negative, you can't help but communicate them to your child.

rent situation—and there is no better weapon to fight depression than hope.

Interpersonal Therapy

Interpersonal therapy focuses on the relationships in a child's life. The counselor might work on providing your child with the skills needed to more effectively communicate and interact with peers and family members. For example, when your child feels stressed, she may respond by yelling or screaming. This usually results in a return volley from the person who's being attacked, creating an unpleasant situation that can escalate out of control. If your child could express that she feels stressed out and overwhelmed without attacking another person, this escalation would fizzle and attention could be paid to helping her feel calmer.

The therapist (and a parent!) might encourage a child to say that she is stressed out and needs a couple of minutes to calm down before the conversation goes any further. This will allow for a de-escalation of emotional intensity, so that she can respond better to the situation. Other skills and strategies that help a child understand her relationships better and interact more positively with others are explored in interpersonal therapy.

Social Skills Training

Ideally, social skills training is done with a group of children, so that a child can practice the skills that are needed to effectively interact and socialize with his peers. This type of counseling is usually best accessed through a child's school, because other children will be available in that setting. However, it's my experience that schools tend to underutilize this therapy or not use it wisely. Creating groups of children who are all socially impaired doesn't work, because nobody in the group can model positive social behavior. Children learn more from behaviors they see being modeled than by having someone tell them what to do. An ideal group would consist of three to five students, several of whom already have relatively good social skills.

Within individual counseling sessions, I find it effective to work with children on scripts that help them learn how to act in various social situations. If you think about it, just as there are scripts for movies or plays, there are also informal and unacknowledged scripts for social situations. If I go to a restaurant, I can expect to be greeted by a host or hostess, be assigned to a table, and be given a menu; choose an appetizer, a main course, and a dessert; get a check; pay a bill; and leave a tip. While there is some variation within this script, it provides a structure, letting me know what I can expect and how I will behave in the restaurant. The same type of preparation might help a child when he goes to school, visits at a new friend's house, attends a party, takes part in a family gathering, and so on. The idea here is to develop a general script so your child will know what to expect and how to behave in a social situation. With this knowledge, he'll probably feel less anxiety and demonstrate more appropriate social skills.

Family Therapy

The psychologist who uses family therapy techniques works with the child and his parents (and, often, siblings and other significant family

Strategies to Improve Social Interactions

- **Give the royal shrug.** I recommend this strategy for a child who is being verbally teased or being called names. I suggest that after the child is teased, she can shrug her shoulders and walk past the other child. I tell the child to imagine that she's a queen and the person doing the teasing is a poor peasant not worth responding to. I tell her to give the name-caller the "royal shrug" and ignore him. The children to whom I've offered this strategy have reported great success using it. It gives a child a means of dealing with teasing without making it worse and getting herself into more trouble.

- **Express anger verbally, not physically.** When I counsel a child who has been acting out physically, I ask him to express in words what action he would typically take in a particular situation. Then we work on finding words to replace the action. For example, if a child hits other people when he is upset, I might suggest that he can say, "I'm so upset I feel like hitting something," instead of actually hitting someone. If he normally throws objects, I might suggest that he can say, "I'm so angry I feel like throwing something." Usually when a child is able to effectively express his feelings, he no longer has to hit or throw objects.

- **Use "I" instead of "you" statements to express feelings.** Saying "I feel upset" in response to an unsettling situation is much more effective than saying "You are making me angry." First, the child is acknowledging her own feelings and accepting that it is she who feels that way. The unstated message she then conveys to herself is that no one else can control her feelings, and it allows her to understand that she has many possible responses to another person's behavior. Also, because the "I" statement isn't perceived by the other person as a challenge, the likelihood of conflict escalating is minimized.

members) to treat the symptoms of depression. Working with parents can have a dramatic impact on a child. In my experience, counseling in the schools is often less effective than private counseling because parents usually aren't brought into the process. A much more complete picture of a child's situation is available to a therapist when he has a chance to meet the family. Parents may be willing to bring up problem situations that a child, for whatever reason, is reluctant to discuss.

One of the important benefits of family counseling is that the therapist can make parents aware that their child is depressed and is not just being difficult and disobedient. Instead of working against their child, they learn to work with him as a team to beat the depression. The irony is that when a child is depressed, he needs his parents more than ever, but he tends to push them away because of his depression. I often work with parents on increasing the support and understanding for the child within the family. Good counseling should lead to increased family flexibility and new ways of dealing with problems.

Behavior Modification

Behavior modification therapy works on structuring the child's environment in order to shape the child's behavior. Part of behavior modification involves setting up a system of rewards and consequences for behavior. The idea is to target behaviors that need to change. The primary source of change then comes from providing rewards ranging from praise to privileges or prizes for demonstrating the achievement of a positive goal. Most behavior plans work on the assumption that the rewards should follow as soon after the demonstration of the desired behaviors as possible.

The premise of behavior modification is that the antecedents (the prior events) and the consequences (the reaction the child gets in response to the events) will shape the child's behavior. Therefore, behavior modification looks at the environmental factors that trigger a child feeling upset and at how people around the child react to her behavior. If you can determine what specific events make things worse for your child, you can try to change those events or prevent them from occurring.

I often find that a depressed child feels the most distress at night before going to sleep. Negative thoughts tend to be most prevalent when the child is not busy with school or otherwise occupied. In this case, the antecedent is downtime with nothing to do, and the consequences are increased negative thoughts and self-deprecation. To counteract this, I often ask a child and his parents to engage in assignments or activities, to counteract the negative thoughts that arise when the child isn't absorbed in something.

Parents can suggest that the child do any of the following:

- Spend time with a parent playing a game or reading a story before going to bed.
- Keep a diary in which the child lists one positive thought, feeling, or action that occurred during the day.
- Use self-talk to reinforce positive traits about herself.
- Create a positive image of a time he felt successful, relaxed, or happy.

Also, you can provide consequences in the form of incentives for promoting behaviors that either fight or minimize the effect of depression. Among the most effective positive consequences, especially if your child is sad and suffering from low self-esteem, are praise and encouragement. When a child hears from a trusted adult that he's done something well, when he is encouraged to try something new and then is praised for taking the chance, that child is being offered a positive consequence for his behavior. As adults, we may have internalized some of those voices that let us say to ourselves, "Wow, that was hard, but I tried and I did a pretty good job of it." Children, especially depressed children, need the reward of actually hearing the words from someone else.

Positive reinforcement, like any other interaction with a child, needs to be offered in an honest and respectful way. Here are some different types of positive reinforcement you might try:

- **Smiles.** Everyone understands the message of a smile. "You've made me happy," your smile says, and that's a powerful reward.
- **Approval comments.** In Little League games all over the country, parents and coaches tell players that they've done a good job at bat or made a great catch. Just a couple of words acknowledging a child's efforts and achievements go a long way.

- **Hugs.** Like smiles, hugs send a message. "You're lovable—I'm really pleased with you," your hug says, and once again you've delivered a powerful reward.
- **Privileges.** A child who has set a goal, followed through, and achieved his goal may be rewarded with a special privilege in recognition of his achievement. If he's done his homework every night for a week, perhaps he'll be rewarded on Friday by being allowed to choose a television show to watch.
- **Concrete physical rewards.** Like privileges, concrete rewards of things—for example, a gold star, a book, or a new CD—may be given for the achievement of a goal. The reward should be kept simple and in proportion to the task, but like the trophies some adults prize in recognition of being top salesperson or most improved bowler, these rewards are an ongoing reminder that something positive has been accomplished and may therefore be significant in injecting some much-needed hope into the outlook of a depressed child.

Parents should carefully evaluate the effect of praise on their child. Some depressed children don't respond well to praise and positive feedback because they don't feel that they deserve it. I once worked with an eleven-year-old boy who actually became more belligerent whenever he received praise. There were two reasons for this negative reaction. First, he didn't feel that he deserved any praise at all because he didn't feel he was a good person. He also felt that the people who were praising him were setting him up by having expectations of him that he couldn't deliver. He was a talented artist, but he became angry if someone complimented one of his drawings. He felt that it put him under pressure to make another drawing that would never be as good as the one he'd just completed.

If your child doesn't respond well to praise, I suggest that you raise this as an issue in a counseling session. As a parent, you don't want to stop praising your child. Instead, you want help to remove the roadblocks that stand in the way of your child's acceptance of praise.

Parents who want to try behavior modification techniques with their children should keep the following principles in mind:

- Focus on the one specific behavior that most interferes with your child's functioning. Don't try to attack too many negative behaviors at the same time. Instead, concentrate on the behavior that causes the most impairment.
- Provide immediate consequences for your child's behaviors. Deal immediately with the inappropriate behavior (using negative consequences) or appropriate behavior (using positive consequences). The longer you wait, the less effective the message you'll send to your child.
- Illustrate your child's progress through the use of a graph. If the graph doesn't show progress, then you need to reevaluate your strategies.
- Constantly revise the type of positive reinforcement your child receives. After a time, the novelty of the reinforcement may wear off, and your child might return to her previous level of performance. This is especially likely for a child who is hyperactive or has difficulty paying attention.

Relaxation Techniques

Since stress is both a cause and a result of depression, a therapist might suggest using relaxation exercises to help decrease the tension a child is carrying in his body. Most of these exercises involve a series of actions in which a child tenses and then gradually relaxes his muscles. Try these exercises yourself after a hard day and see what a difference they make in how you feel!

Deep Breathing
1. Take a deep breath and slowly let the air out through your nose.
2. As you breathe in, slowly raise your hands until they are over your head. Stretch your hands as far as they can go. Hold your breath a second or two and then slowly let the air out while gradually lowering your hands. Repeat this activity once more.
3. Now close your eyes and place your hands in your lap. Notice how effortlessly the air goes into and out of your lungs.

Isometrics

1. While keeping the rest of your body relaxed, squeeze the fingers of your right hand together to make a fist. Gradually squeeze tighter and tighter. Notice the tension, and then as you let go, release all your anger and frustration. Focus on your hand and how relaxed it is. Repeat.
2. Now make a fist with your left hand and gradually make it tighter. Feel the tension and let go of it. Notice how your hand feels when it is relaxed. Repeat.
3. You can add new groups of muscles by clenching the muscles of your arms, your shoulders, your feet, your legs, even your face, until you feel the tension, and then let go.

These relaxation techniques help release stress, promote calm, and allow a child to feel more in control of her own behavior.

Education

As part of a therapeutic strategy, education helps a child and the other important people in her life better understand what's happening and what can be expected. Depression is so often misunderstood, thought—wrongly!—to be a moral weakness or a character flaw. Too many people don't realize that depression is a biological predisposition to having difficulty dealing with stress. Children often don't know why they're depressed and come up with explanations that aren't helpful in treating it. A depressed child may view the depression as being a weakness and blame himself for the negative feelings. Rather than seeing it as a personal failing, he needs to view depression as an illness that can be successfully treated.

Parents may find it useful to share knowledge of a child's depression with his teachers, so that the people who see him every day in school can better understand his problems. It's easier for a teacher to be kind and patient to a student when he knows that her problem behavior is really an expression of the child's depression. Children who are depressed are often difficult to be around and are easily irritated by negative experiences. An increased understanding of a child's depression can help prevent a continuation of the negative cycle at home and school.

Psychoanalytic Therapy

Counselors who engage in psychoanalytic therapy work under the assumption that past events are the subterranean source of current problems. The psychologist may lead you back through your past with the idea that unconscious conflicts are the cause of depression. In order for a person to feel better, psychoanalytic therapists believe that the individual has to develop some insight into the nature of these conflicts. Most psychologists today are not trained under this model. Psychoanalytic counseling is long term and doesn't appear to be any more effective than other types of counseling that take considerably less time and effort. Some people may still think that psychologists all resemble Sigmund Freud because of the impact of movies and television, but it's unlikely that the counseling available for your child will consist of him lying on a couch and talking about memories of his past.

Play Therapy

Play therapy is used by many therapists to build rapport with a child. In my experience, play is the best way to reach a young child. Many therapists use feeling or self-expression games to get to know a child and initiate discussions in a nonthreatening format. Playing a game together is often a means of reducing a child's anxiety level and making her more comfortable with the counseling process. In fact, for some children, engaging in play activity with a therapist is necessary before they can be comfortable enough to discuss the issues that are bothering them.

A strict interpretation of play therapy tends to follow a psychoanalytic model, requiring that the therapist give the child the opportunity to work out his problems in play. Theoretically, play allows the child to gain insight into his past. For example, if the child has been traumatized, he'll take that trauma with him into his play. The therapist then uses play to help the child learn to work out the trauma within the safety of the counseling session. The tools of play therapy in this model often consist of sandboxes or Play-Doh, which the child can manipulate.

However, many therapists (including me) use play simply as a way to develop rapport with a child and make him comfortable communicating his feelings. I don't expect the child to take me back to the scene of some otherwise unknown trauma. Instead, I use play as a bridge to make a good connection with the child, allowing him to express difficult emotions and work through problems more easily.

Hospitalization

Hospitalization as therapy is an option for children who are at risk of hurting themselves or others or who are excessively noncompliant or aggressive. The central issue is safety. Hospitalization should only be considered when a mental health professional feels that a child is not safe.

Getting a child hospitalized is a difficult process, one that a family and a child will never forget and one that may lead to a heightened sense of insecurity. A child who is hospitalized may have never been away from his parents before, and he may become insecure and worry about when he'll be able to return home. Even when he comes back home, he might have increased fears about going back to the hospital and coping with another separation from his parents, siblings, and friends. A child who has been hospitalized realizes that he can be taken out of his home at any time, without his permission, for an unpredictable length of time, and all of it is out of his control.

However, there may be several advantages to hospitalization. Perhaps the biggest advantage is that the child can be professionally monitored for any reactions to medication and can receive ongoing care from experienced providers who have resources to help the most troubled children. As a secondary outcome, such an action can give parent and child a time to recharge and explore alternative ways of dealing with the problems that led to the unsafe situation. An aggressive child may eventually feel reassured to know that there are effective limits to his acting out behavior and be grateful for the help in preventing harm to himself or others.

A Plan for Parents

► Take notes at your child's counseling sessions so that you remember the important points that were discussed and the strategies you can use to help your child feel better.

► Bring an appointment book to your counseling sessions so it's easier for you to remember the date of the next appointment and to make sure you don't have any conflicts.

► Keep a log of your child's progress in meeting goals that have been set up in counseling.

► Try to call your therapist at least a day ahead of time if you have to cancel an appointment.

5

Medication Options
for Depression

LET'S FACE IT—of all the topics in this book, this is the one that parents are most confused about. And with good reason, because each day, new studies about antidepressants are reported in the media, lawmakers pass new legislation, and parents who want to make wise and informed decisions about how to help their children become healthy get dizzy from the barrage of information, half-information, and unsubstantiated information.

I want to help you navigate these turbulent waters, but I also hope you understand that no book can diagnose a child's illness and prescribe a proper course of treatment. It takes a living, breathing person, maybe even a team of people, to do that properly. What I can do is help you make better sense of what the current studies show, what they mean, and how to apply that knowledge to your own family's situation.

First, you should understand that my opinions and interpretations are based on my years of experience, on reading the current journals and papers, and on my belief that data needs to be understood before it can be applied to real life.

Next, you should keep in mind that because each child, indeed each human being, is unique and complex and because medical science, including our knowledge of mental health, is still imperfect, unpredictable things happen. Perhaps only one person in a million will break out in a rash when taking a simple over-the-counter painkiller—but if you're that person, you still itch. And the consequences with some of these medications may be much more distressing than temporary skin discomfort.

Also, I urge you to try to put aside your worries and read this section with an open mind, do more research, and consult with a physician if you have questions about the use of medications to treat your child's depression.

Finally, please remember that most people, including the majority of mental health professionals, would prefer to treat a child's depression without medication where that's possible. Only in cases where counseling and other strategies haven't led to improvement, or in cases in which the initial depression is so severe it's unlikely that a child will respond positively without medication, do most physicians and psychologists include drugs as part of the child's treatment.

If a child's depression can be effectively treated through counseling, education, and the application of strategies at home and at school that help him overcome the debilitating effects of his illness, everyone would be delighted. Parents would feel pleased that they don't have to be concerned about the issues that have been raised, and mental health professionals would be glad that a positive outcome was achieved without any of the uncertainties that prescribing medications carries.

However, many mental health professionals have found that medication can be an effective tool when a child's depression is significant and other strategies have proven unsuccessful.

The key to achieving good results with antidepressant medication is good monitoring. I wish I could print this in neon.

If your child is on medication, I urge you to work with both a physician (a child psychiatrist, pediatrician, or family physician) and a mental health professional with expertise and experience in monitoring the side effects of medications.

Several highly publicized studies have indicated that some children may experience an increase in suicidal thoughts while taking antidepressant medication. As of the time I wrote this book, it's important to note that, among all the studies I'm familiar with, no child has actually committed suicide.

Although there have been occasional anecdotal reports of suicide with some of these antidepressant medications, no linking cause and effect has been demonstrated.

These studies are in the exploratory stage, and they led the FDA in October of 2004 to recommend that warnings be placed on the packages of all antidepressant medication, whether for children, adolescents, or adults. The FDA reviewed twenty-four studies involving 4,400 children taking antidepressants for various conditions, such as depression, anxiety, and obsessive-compulsive disorder. The preliminary findings suggest that 3 percent of children taking these medications reported increased suicidal thinking.

Although none of these studies proposes a clear reason for the reported 3 percent increase in suicidal thinking, my best understanding is that this increase is due to medication side effects. My analysis of these studies is that a small percentage of children may, in fact, become worse through the use of antidepressant medications. However, the great majority of children do report a lessening of depressed feelings and negative thoughts.

A recent study conducted by the National Institute of Mental Health, published in the *Journal of the American Medical Association* in August 2004, involved 439 children aged twelve to seventeen who were randomly assigned to treatment of Prozac alone, cognitive behavioral therapy alone, a combination of the two treatments, or a placebo pill. The study found that adolescents with moderate to severe depression did best when receiving a combination of Prozac and cognitive behavioral therapy, with 71 percent showing some improvement. In addition, 60 percent of the children taking Prozac alone showed improvement—superior results when compared to the use of cognitive behavioral therapy alone, for which 43 percent of the children experienced improvement.

This was one of the first studies in the research literature to demonstrate the clinical effectiveness of medications. This study also found that suicidal thinking, which was present for 29 percent of the children at the beginning of the study, significantly *declined* after the children had taken the prescribed medication.

Another interesting finding in this study was that the use of a placebo (that is, a sugar pill with no medication) led to an improvement rate of 34 percent. Just being in a treatment situation of any kind that a child believes in can lead to some positive results.

One of the major concerns of the FDA is that children who are being prescribed antidepressants may not be receiving good monitoring by their physicians—and by their parents. One of the goals of this book is to increase parents' knowledge of antidepressant medications so that they can make informed decisions and develop an increased awareness of what to look for regarding side effects.

It's critical that parents learn about the possible side effects of medication and understand the warning signs that something dangerous may be happening, so that a child can be identified and not put at greater risk if he should be one of the 3 percent who experiences increased suicidal thinking.

Because the next several chapters deal with medication and its appropriate use, many of the cases I'll discuss involve children who did need medication. Please keep in mind that it's always my first choice, and the first choice of most mental health professionals, to treat a child without having to use medication.

Potential Side Effects of Antidepressant Medication

Tom's story is a vivid example of the kind of side effects mentioned in recent studies. The events were, for me, unusual in that I haven't had a lot of experience with such side effects in my years in private practice and as a school psychologist. What happened brought home to me the realities of some things that I had advocated in theory but hadn't seen firsthand.

▶   Tom was a fifteen-year-old-boy who had experienced a significant depression for at least a year and a half before he came to my office. He came from a good home and was both academically and athletically talented. He didn't know why he felt sad all the time, and after several weeks of counseling, only minor progress was made in helping lift his depression.

I called his physician to recommend a trial of antidepressant medication, and Tom was placed on 25 mg of Zoloft, which led to an initial mild improvement.

As we continued counseling, I concluded that Tom's symptoms weren't improving much, so I again called his physician after six weeks to discuss an increase in medication. Tom was then placed on 50 mg of Zoloft and reported feeling much better after a week.

However, after two weeks, he told his parents that he'd had the urge to kill himself during swim practice. He didn't really want to die, and so he cut out of swim practice because he was afraid he would drown himself. He was deeply scared when he shared this information with his parents. His father called me that day, and I scheduled an emergency visit that night. I suggested that he no longer take 50 mg of Zoloft and contacted his physician to suggest a change of medication. Tom is now on 10 mg of Prozac. He doesn't have any side effects and is making good progress in our counseling sessions.

I made sure to let Tom and his parents know that my practice has a twenty-four-hour hotline that is covered at all times by a mental health professional who is part of my practice. We all take turns carrying a beeper, so someone is always within easy reach. I told Tom to call at any time if he experienced this problem again or one like it. Thankfully, he hasn't needed to do this. But if Tom hadn't told his parents, or if his parents had delayed in contacting me, or if I hadn't responded to my messages, or any one of a lot of other *ifs*, the ending of this story might be very different.

Please keep in mind these two important points:

- **Side effects can develop at any time during a course of treatment.**
- **All children on medication need to be actively monitored.**

Most of the side effects are behavioral in nature and may not be noticed by your child's pediatrician. After all, parents, siblings, teachers, and friends are the ones who have everyday contact with a child, who can see that a child who had been calm or even lethargic is suddenly agitated and angry.

The Importance of Careful Monitoring

Arthur's case provides an example of a common problem that might occur without careful monitoring. Parents should be aware that some behavior that might appear to be willfully disobedient or aggressive may be medication side effects. Rather than requiring discipline, a child may need a change in medication or in dosage.

▶ Arthur was a nine-year-old child who was referred to me by his pediatrician because he exhibited symptoms of depression. Although he was truly sad and unhappy, there appeared to be no environmental trigger for his feelings. His parents provided a loving and caring home for him, and he wasn't dealing with any major stresses. However, there was a strong family history of depression, and he seemed to share this genetic predisposition.

His parents reported that he had been sad for many months, was doing poorly in school, and had stopped socializing with his friends. He often cried about how unhappy he was but could never say what was bothering him. I saw Arthur for several counseling sessions, but we made little progress. I tried to get him to participate in assignments at home geared to reducing his depression, including exercise, making positive comments to himself, and working at expressing his feelings. We also started a behavior modification plan to give him more incentives to do his schoolwork and to participate in social situations, but Arthur was unresponsive.

After several weeks, I contacted his pediatrician about starting him on antidepressant medication. He was placed on 10 mg of Paxil, and after two weeks, he made remarkable improvement. He started to feel better and seemed to be his old self again. He no longer cried so frequently and was doing well in school. We started to lower the frequency of our sessions after six weeks but didn't cut off the counseling altogether. I let a month pass between visits, and he continued to do well. I then scheduled another visit in a month, and he continued to show excellent progress. Therefore, I scheduled our next visit for six weeks later.

At his six-week visit, Arthur was no longer doing well. He had become extremely impulsive and was engaging in chronic stealing and lying. He was also more aggressive with his siblings. I was concerned that his antidepressant medication might be a factor in his misbehavior. One of the possible side effects of antidepressant medication is disinhibition.

In this situation, a child appears to lose good control over his impulses and engages in inappropriate behaviors without concern about the consequences. It's as if the brakes in his car have stopped working properly. Because of my concern and the fact that Arthur wasn't showing signs of depression, I contacted his pediatrician again to suggest taking him off the Paxil, and he agreed.

When I saw Arthur two weeks later, his inappropriate behaviors were gone and his depression had passed—and he didn't need medication at that time. I had not only helped Arthur through counseling and consulting with his doctor about starting him on medication, but I also made sure to schedule periodic counseling sessions just to check in.

Starting and Stopping Antidepressant Medication for Children

When dealing with children, most physicians and psychiatrists start with a half dose of adult levels of medication and build up. With preadolescent children, because of their lower body weight, I believe the prudent approach is to start at a quarter dose, unless the depression is severe.

With many of these medications, it may take several weeks before they produce a desired change. It's not like taking an antacid for an upset stomach and counting on relief within an hour. The chemical changes that the medications produce don't happen quite so quickly, so it's important to be patient until the medication is established in the child's body.

For most children on antidepressant medications, their mood becomes better and their symptoms of depression are alleviated within about a month. Sometimes the medication needs to be changed or adjusted, but most children will feel some type of benefit when properly medicated. However, approximately 20 percent of depressed children are resistant to the benefits of these medications. This is a frustrating situation for the child, the parents, and the doctors providing treatment. In this situation, a physician may prescribe several different medications in the hope that one will help. If nothing seems to help, the next step should be to take the child to a psychiatrist, so that a combination of medications can be explored.

In the beginning, and all through the time a child is on antide-pressant medication (as you've seen in the cases of Arthur and Tom), you must work with a mental health professional and a physician to make sure that your child is being properly monitored for side effects.

It's important to note that these medications shouldn't be stopped abruptly. When people take an antidepressant medication, their nervous systems get used to having the extra supply of serotonin, and an abrupt change can be like flipping the "off" switch when you're on a roller coaster ride. People may get sick or develop flulike symptoms when antidepressant medication is stopped without a weaning-off process.

Despite the evidence that medications can be effective in treating depression, no scientific evidence exists to determine which child should take which type of medication. Because people's nervous systems differ, it's not yet possible for doctors to tell with certainty which medication would be best for a particular person. Many of the medications are similar. The one prescribed for initial treatment might simply be the personal preference of the treating physician, based upon her past experiences with a particular drug. Very often, a physician will also look at what medications other members in a child's family have used when being treated for depression. If a parent or sibling has responded well to one type of medication, that might be the best one to start with.

Medications and Dosages

Several categories of medications are typically prescribed to treat childhood depression. Each category works on a different biochemical principle, and each requires careful, thoughtful monitoring.

Selective Serotonin Reuptake Inhibitors (SSRIs)

The most common class of medications used to treat depression is the selective serotonin reuptake inhibitors (SSRIs). These medications can take up to a month to achieve a full therapeutic effect. However, a child usually sees some improvement by the second week. SSRIs work on the brain by increasing the supply of the neurotransmitter serotonin. Having more serotonin increases a person's ability to deal with stress. The SSRI antidepressants, and Wellbutrin and Effexor, are not known to cause damage to one's body organs. Therefore, if a child is taking them, periodic blood work isn't necessary.

Please be especially cautious if your physician prescribes an SSRI-type medication to a child under puberty. The disinhibition effect that I described with Arthur is very common. In fact, about a third of young children I work with experience this side effect. It can be a serious problem if a child becomes worse on antidepressant medication and nobody is monitoring the situation. A prescribing physician probably will schedule a review appointment in three to four weeks—but the problems can manifest in a matter of days.

The prescribing physician, of course, won't be able to help you and your child if he doesn't get feedback from you regarding changes in your child's behavior. Therefore, if your child is placed on this type of medication, it's critical that you have a mechanism for reporting problems to the prescribing physician. Some physicians aren't aware of this disinhibition effect or treat reports of such behavior lightly. Because of the focus of their training, they're more likely to pay attention to physical rather than behavioral side effects. And if a child is being treated at a clinic, a phone call may be forwarded after hours to an on-call physician who doesn't know the child. Having a psychologist or social worker involved when a problem arises usually leads to more personal monitoring and provides an extra safety check. I check my voice mail every day and will personally get back to a family if there's a question or concern.

- **Prozac.** This was the first of these antidepressants and is currently the only antidepressant approved for children by the FDA. Although the FDA has approved only Prozac, physicians and psychiatrists still routinely prescribe other brands of antidepressant medication, and it is not illegal to do so. Prozac has a starting dose of 10 to 20 mg a day. I often suggest that a pediatrician explore the use of a 5 mg dose for a preadolescent child.

Prozac tends to last a long time in a person's body. It probably takes longer to get into a child's nervous system than any of the other antidepressant medications, in many cases as long as four weeks to achieve its full effect. In some ways, this might be a good thing, since the slower start-up may lead to a gentler experience with fewer side effects.

The 2004 FDA finding and subsequent approval of Prozac seem to have increased its use among children. Preliminary studies have also suggested that it may have less of an effect on suicidal ideation than other medications. Prozac comes in liquid form, making it easier to administer to children who have difficulty swallowing pills. A sustained-release version of Prozac is also available. Instead of taking the medication every day, a child takes it once a week. This can be a good choice for children who are resistant to taking medication on a daily basis. However, this type of Prozac doesn't appear to be as effective as the daily version.

Because of the FDA findings and my own personal positive experiences with children taking Prozac, I tend to recommend it as a good first option for a child who will be prescribed antidepressants.

- **Zoloft.** This medication has a starting dose of 25 to 50 mg and has been a common choice for children and adolescents. Like Prozac, it can take up to four weeks to become effective, but it tends not to stay as long in one's body as Prozac when the child is being weaned off the medication.
- **Paxil.** This medication has a starting dose of 10 to 20 mg. The newer Paxil CR has a continual release format that may have fewer side effects. The starting dose is 12.5 to 25 mg. It should be noted that Paxil had fallen out of favor for a while with several physicians in my area, since it was the first medication on which the FDA placed a caution because of previously cited data associating it with increased suicidal ideation in children. However, this may change now that the same caution has been put on all antidepressants.
- **Celexa.** This medication has a starting dose of 10 to 20 mg. Celexa has the advantage of achieving a therapeutic level within

two weeks. The only negative issue I find with it is that it may be more sedating than the other medications.

- **Lexapro.** This is one of the newer medications and is basically new and improved Celexa, with a starting dose of 10 mg.

Other Antidepressants

Just as the SSRIs work on serotonin, other antidepressants affect different neurotransmitters in the brain.

- **Wellbutrin.** This antidepressant works on the neurotransmitter dopamine. Having more available dopamine can result in a child having more self-control and feeling better. Typically, Wellbutrin is prescribed in a sustained-release format and comes in 100 and 150 mg doses that a child takes twice a day. The sustained-release version tends to be a lot more effective and has fewer side effects than the older, shorter-acting version of the drug.

  Someone with an already existing seizure disorder *should not* take Wellbutrin. Otherwise, it is a safe medication that isn't toxic and doesn't require blood tests. Wellbutrin is also a second-line treatment for ADHD because of its mild positive effect on attention span.

  Recently, a newer version came out: Wellbutrin XL, a sustained-plus release one-a-day formula. This is a positive improvement over the regular sustained-release version. The only negative is that some insurance companies have been slow to cover it, since it is more expensive than the older Wellbutrin SR version. The Wellbutrin XL comes in 150 and 300 mg doses.

- **Effexor.** This antidepressant works on both serotonin and dopamine. It tends to be more effective for anxiety and obsessive-compulsive disorder and is not usually the first choice to treat depression. The typical starting dose is 37.5 mg and can go up to 150 mg, although I know of at least one case in which 300 mg was given to an adult. At smaller doses, Effexor tends to have minimal side effects. With Effexor, it is important to monitor blood pressure, especially for high doses.

Tricyclic Antidepressants

Examples of tricyclic antidepressants are amitriptyline, desipramine, and imipramine. Because some severe health risks may be associated with their use, I suggest trying to avoid these medications, although they may be tried under the supervision of a good psychiatrist, after all other medication options have proven ineffective. Several children reportedly have died of heart failure as a result of taking these medications, and although the numbers account for less than 1 percent of the children who have been prescribed these medications, I would use tricyclic antidepressants only when other possibilities have been exhausted.

Natural Herbs or Supplements

Some herbs, like Saint-John's-wort, are used to treat depression, but their effectiveness is unclear. While initial research indicated that Saint-John's-wort may be effective for mild to moderate depression, recent research indicates that its effectiveness may not be significant. The typical dose for an adult is 100 mg three times a day. No guidelines exist for its use in children.

Placebo Effect

Some people acquire fake pills that have no active ingredient and tell their child he is taking a medication to reduce depression. They believe that the child will get better because he believes the pills will help him. While some children may benefit from this procedure, placebos don't work nearly as well as the real thing. Furthermore, I don't believe that it's beneficial in the long run to mislead or trick your child, since this may damage the trust he's placed in you. That said, it has been demonstrated that telling a child or an adult that he's taking a pill to help him feel less depressed will lead to improvement in 25 to 30 percent of cases. This suggests that a child's beliefs or expectations about becoming better can play a big role in his fight against depression.

Monitoring for Side Effects

Whatever medication might be prescribed for your child, you must monitor her for possible side effects. It's not enough to say, "Oh, if something's wrong, the doctor will find it." When your child is on antidepressant medication, it becomes part of your job description as a parent to watch her behavior more carefully, because the consequences of ignoring side effects can be grave.

Some side effects may be mild and transitory but should still be reported to your child's pediatrician or psychiatrist. These include stomachaches or headaches. Often, these problems go away, but if they persist, you need to notify your child's doctor. Some children experience increased tiredness. Some parents have had success in having their child take her medicine in the evening instead of in the morning. Because you don't want to sedate your child, it may be necessary to try a different medication if the problem persists. On the other hand, some children report sleep disturbances in the form of extremely vivid or strange dreams when taking medication. Often, this goes away on its own. However, if it persists and the child is upset about it, this might be good cause to explore a change in medication. Finally, weight gain, which may be an especially important issue for an adolescent concerned about his or her physical appearance, might prompt you to consult the prescribing physician about alternative medications.

There's another possible side effect related to the use of SSRIs that people—including some physicians—often don't talk about: decreased sex drive or sexual performance. This side effect is the major reason why adults frequently take themselves off SSRI medications. While this isn't an issue for elementary school–aged children, it may be an issue for older adolescents. Although uncommon among adolescents, especially those on low doses of medication, decreased sex drive or sexual performance can be very embarrassing for adolescents if it does happen. To make matters more complicated, most adolescents are uncomfortable talking about this problem. Not many teenage boys or girls are willing to discuss their active sex lives with their parents. When I work with an adolescent who will be taking an

SSRI, I usually bring this up in private. I ask him to tell me privately at some later point in time if he feels this problem has become an issue so that we can discuss possible remedies.

Side Effects That Indicate a Need to Change Medication or Dosage

While some side effects are mild and may even become less noticeable over time, others are indicators of more serious concerns requiring a change in dosage or medication. If your child experiences the side effects described in the following list, you should consult with her doctor about the possibility of lowering or changing her medication:

- **Being overly silly or uninhibited.** This is the disinhibition I mentioned earlier, a common side effect in young children. When a child exhibits this symptom, she can be difficult to be around, since her impulsivity and silliness can be annoying. But disinhibition can lead to inappropriate and even dangerous behavior and is a signal that medication or dosage needs to be changed.
- **Aggressive behavior.** This is a clear signal that the medication doesn't agree with your child and that alternatives should be explored. I've worked with several children who were normally well behaved but began to have problems with aggressive behavior shortly after taking a new medication. When the medication was withdrawn, the behavior returned to normal. Without good monitoring, a child might exhibit aggressive behavior for a relatively long period of time, which is likely to lead to social and academic difficulties in school.
- **Hyperactive behavior.** Being on an antidepressant shouldn't make a child hyperactive. In Chapter 7, I'll explore bipolar disorder, a serious illness that may be made worse by antidepressant medication if it isn't recognized and properly treated. Not all children who become hyperactive after taking antidepressant medication will be diagnosed with bipolar disorder, but such changes in a child's behavior indicate that the medication needs to be changed.

- **Increased anxiety and irritability.** Sometimes medications have the opposite effect than was intended. An increase in anxiety and irritability is one of the side effects that concerns me most, because it might be a factor in the increased suicidal ideation that was described in some of the studies. If you notice these changes in your child, you should contact your physician or psychiatrist at once.
- **Shaking of legs or hands.** This isn't a common side effect, but if it occurs, you should contact your child's physician.

Compliance Concerns

The SSRI medications, as well as Wellbutrin and Effexor, need to be taken every day to be effective. Not only is regular use important for their effectiveness, but suddenly stopping the medication might cause a child to feel sick and develop flulike symptoms. A child might not like the idea of taking medication because he may feel that if he's taking medication, then something terrible must be wrong with him. Children, especially adolescents, don't want to feel different from their friends and classmates. They may also interpret taking medication as a sign of weakness. They may believe that they should be able to feel better without taking a medication. For some children, the idea of taking any medication makes them uncomfortable because they worry about the effects that medications will have on their body.

Taking medication can also lead to a power struggle between the child and his parents. I have worked with several children who would take their medication at school but refuse to take it at home. Sometimes a child will refuse to take his medication as a way of telling his parents that he's the boss and they can't control what he does. If this happens, the issue should be addressed in counseling.

Most medication compliance issues can be avoided if the child is actively involved in the process of making the decision to take a medication. If you try to force a child to take a medication without her agreement, medication compliance issues are likely to follow. The child should be informed about possible side effects and should be reassured that she won't be asked to continue to take a medication that makes her feel uncomfortable. That is probably the most reassuring thing that you can do for a child taking a medication. This assurance gives a child some control over the situation.

However, as in other parenting matters, giving a child total control over the situation isn't in his best interest. If he truly needs to be on a medication, you need to let your child know that other medications that don't have uncomfortable side effects will continue to be explored.

Some children are resistant to taking medication because they just hate the idea of taking or swallowing pills. In this situation, it may help to use a liquid version or crush the pill and put it in applesauce or some other food that will make swallowing it more palatable to your child. But I strongly caution you not to do this unless you tell your child what you're doing. If she finds out that you've tricked her, it may damage the trust between you and make the issue of taking a medication a more difficult one.

A Plan for Parents

▶ Be sure to keep reading about antidepressant medications in newspapers and on the Internet. Medical knowledge is being updated at a dizzying pace.

▶ If a physician or psychiatrist recommends medication for your child's depression, be sure to discuss any possible side effects.

▶ Take notice of behavioral changes in your child, and take extra time to talk to him, as a way of monitoring progress.

▶ If you notice changes in your child's behavior, contact her therapist or physician right away. If you must leave a message, make sure your message is clear, and be persistent. You should have telephone contact within twenty-four hours at most.

6

Depression and Other
Mental Health Issues

UNFORTUNATELY, CHILDREN WITH depression may have other mental health conditions that need treatment. If a therapist or parent only focuses on the symptoms of depression and ignores the other mental health conditions, a child won't receive effective treatment. It's like having an earache and a stomachache at the same time—they require different treatment in order to help the person being treated to become truly healthy.

We call the other mental health issues comorbid disorders. A child who is depressed may well be suffering from ADHD, anxiety, obsessive-compulsive disorder, or substance abuse issues at the same time. Or he might be experiencing bipolar disorder, which is discussed separately in Chapter 7.

The Jones family, with whom I worked for several years, provides several examples of children for whom depression and other mental health disorders coexist—and they also offer hope that help can be found for many such children.

▶ **A Family with Multiple Mental Health Problems**

Mr. and Mrs. Jones had four children. Nick Jones worked at a factory and earned enough money to allow the family a comfortable middle-class life. Emily Jones stayed at home to raise the children. Nick and Emily were very anxious people, and Emily described herself as being hyperactive when she was younger. When he first came to my office, Nick exhibited anxious behavior. His leg continually shook during our session, and he had difficulty making eye contact. His voice drifted off at the end of each sentence.

I first met the Jones family when their oldest son, Danny, who was seventeen, was referred to me because he wasn't attending school. As I spoke with Danny and his parents, I realized that his symptoms were more severe than school officials realized. He never went anywhere by himself, never talked on the telephone, and had to call his mother every twenty minutes when he was at someone's house. I diagnosed Danny with generalized anxiety disorder.

We started counseling, but Danny's positive responses to the counseling strategies were minimal. After several weeks, I contacted his pediatrician to explore the use of an SSRI to treat his anxiety, since SSRIs often reduce stress and anxiety levels as well as treat depression. Danny started on a low dose of Paxil and experienced a mild improvement. However, when the medication dosage was increased, the symptoms showed no further improvement. I had previously had a good experience with Effexor with a child whose symptoms were similar to Danny's. When his pediatrician put him on 37.5 mg of Effexor, Danny experienced an astounding change. He was able to go to school and even go into a store on his own for the first time. In a short time, he had a girlfriend, found a job, and began a whole new social life. I had never seen such a tremendous change in a person.

His parents and his physician were also amazed.

As I wrapped up my last session with Danny, his parents mentioned that his fifteen-year-old sister, Tara, wasn't doing well in school and constantly fought with her siblings. As is often the case, they were so focused on Danny that they couldn't give their attention to Tara until her brother's symptoms were under control. Because of her irritability and recent poor performance in school, I administered a depression scale to assess Tara for depression. She scored in the severely depressed range. Tara reported having thoughts of killing herself and said that the only reason she didn't act on those thoughts was because she didn't want to hurt her parents.

Tara knew that something was wrong with her, but she didn't understand why she felt terrible all the time. While she was a little anxious, she

didn't appear to be as nervous as her older brother. S̶
change in Danny and hoped that something could be done

Tara was very sad and had lost the few friends that she'd
didn't want to fight with her siblings, but her constant irritability
that even the little things they did upset her. She couldn't concentrat̶
school and was failing all her classes. Relieved to be able to express some
of her feelings during counseling, she showed mild improvement. However, given the severity of her depression, I contacted her physician and
she was placed on Zoloft. After she was on Zoloft for several weeks, her
depression began to lift, but she made minimal progress, even when the
dosage was increased. I contacted her physician, and Tara was switched to
Prozac with excellent results. Her parents noticed a big change in her. She
started to do better in school, and even her siblings found that she was
more pleasant to be around. Eventually, she made such good progress that
the medication was discontinued, and we reduced the frequency of her
counseling sessions.

After treating Tara, her parents mentioned that their twelve-year-old
son, Andrew, was also experiencing a lot of anxiety. We set up an appointment for me to meet with Andrew, and it was clear that his symptoms
were different from his brother's and sister's. While he was anxious, he was
not as anxious as Danny. His level of depression was only mild to moderate, instead of being severe. The central issue for Andrew was that he
was suffering from obsessive-compulsive disorder (OCD). He was afraid
that his father would get into a car accident and insisted on driving with
him to work every morning to make sure he'd be all right. He had to blink
seven times when looking someone in the eye. If he didn't do this, he was
afraid something bad would happen to him. His siblings and parents knew
he had some strange behaviors, but they didn't have a clue about the reason for them.

Like Tara, Andrew felt tremendous relief when he shared his feelings
and his actions without someone thinking he was crazy. I told him that
he had symptoms of OCD and assured him that he wasn't crazy. I let him
know that I had worked with other children who had similar problems.
But Andrew was resistant to the cognitive behavioral methods I tried in
counseling sessions. Even though he knew his thoughts weren't rational,
he couldn't stop them. His physician put him on Effexor, hoping it would
help him, as it had helped Danny. However, the Effexor didn't produce

drew was placed on a higher dose, he became
Prozac, which did have positive results. He
mg of Prozac, and his symptoms subsided.
nd Andrew began to do better in school and
wever, his obsessions and compulsions didn't
become more aware of them and knew that
ey no longer impeded his ability to function.
e Jones children exhibited symptoms of the
most common mental health issue that leads parents to seek help for their children: ADHD.

Other Mental Health Issues

Other mental health conditions may exist at the same time as depression or may be confused with depression. Reaching a proper diagnosis is an important part of treatment and will affect decisions about appropriate counseling and medication.

Attention Deficit/Hyperactivity Disorder

Attention Deficit/Hyperactivity Disorder (ADHD) is the primary reason that many parents, doctors, and teachers refer children to me. The symptoms of ADHD include the inability to sustain attention, high levels of activity, and impulsivity. A child with ADHD behaves in ways that get him noticed more frequently than a child with depression. It is believed that 3 to 5 percent of all children will exhibit symptoms of ADHD by the age of seven. As with depression, ADHD appears to be a highly inheritable condition. A parent with ADHD has a 30 percent probability of having a child with its symptoms.

ADHD can be divided into two types. One is called ADHD-combined type, with all the symptoms of inattention, hyperactivity, and impulsivity. There is also another type, called ADHD-predominantly inattentive type. In this situation, the only issue of concern is inattention. The child diagnosed with the predominantly inattentive type of ADHD is not hyperactive or impulsive.

Problems with paying attention have an impact on a child's ability to follow directions, complete schoolwork, and study for tests. Inattention is a major factor when students don't succeed in school. Sound familiar? If a child is depressed, the problem of sustaining attention is one of the things parents might notice first. Being unable to pay attention can cause a child great stress because she can't meet the demands for being successful in school. She might be bright and have good academic skills yet still fail her classes because she can't sustain attention long enough to complete her homework and study for tests.

It is possible for a child to have both depression and ADHD. So how can you sort out the two conditions so that your child can get proper treatment?

The Differences Between ADHD and Depression. We know that both conditions describe children who have difficulty paying attention. While a child with ADHD is impulsive, one with depression is generally irritable and impatient. The depressed child may be impatient because of his irritability and because he doesn't care about the consequences of his actions, while the child with ADHD is impatient because he has poor impulse control and doesn't think about the consequences of his actions before engaging in them.

The main visible difference between ADHD and depression is that of hyperactivity, which is not a factor in depression. Depressed children, in fact, tend to be less active than their peers.

One similarity between children experiencing ADHD and depression is the tendency to focus on immediate as opposed to long-term needs. While each child is more focused with the here and now rather than the future, the child with ADHD can't put her attention on the future because of distraction and impulse control issues, while the depressed child doesn't focus on the future because he views it as being negative and he has no hope.

In order to distinguish between ADHD-predominantly inattentive type and depression, it's important to determine when the symptoms of inattention first occurred. If a child has always exhibited problems with focus and attention, then a counselor might be pretty comfortable attributing the behavior to ADHD. However, if the symptoms are new and the child has paid attention very well in the past, then it's more likely that problems with focus are related to depression. This is one reason why a review of a child's history is so important in making a diagnosis of a mental health condition.

Counseling and Medication for ADHD. Problems with paying attention usually don't respond well to behavior modification strategies. Counseling can help a child and her parents understand how the illness affects the child and then offer ways to develop organizational skills. However, in most cases in which a diagnosis of ADHD is reached, the child will be placed on medication. These drugs, when properly prescribed and monitored, can make an enormous difference in a child's ability to function well in school and in other activities that require focus and concentration. They have few health side effects (which are discussed a little later) while the child is taking them and no apparent long-term side effects. They aren't addicting, which means that a child can stop taking them during weekends and vacations, if he and his parents and physician want to do that.

Interestingly, children who take these medications appear less likely to abuse illegal substances when they get older. A study funded by the National Institute on Drug Abuse and published in the January 2002 issue of *Pediatrics* magazine showed that the use of stimulant medication cut the risk of substance abuse in half. The study, conducted by Tim Wilens through Harvard University, compared the long-term effects of taking medication with 674 subjects who took stimulants versus 360 who weren't medicated.

The stimulants prescribed for ADHD work by increasing the production of neurotransmitters, such as dopamine and norepinephrine, in the frontal lobe of the brain. The neurotransmitters are like mail carriers sending messages to the brain cells. The lack of dopamine and norepinephrine leads to a less active brain that has more difficulty sustaining attention and regulating activity level and impulsivity. Several years ago, research was conducted with adults with ADHD in Scandinavia. A radioactive dye was injected into their brains, and a functional MRI was conducted. The study found that when these adults took stimulant medication, the frontal lobe area of the brain became more alert and active. Researchers attributed the increase in neurotransmitter production to the use of the medication.

The most commonly used medications to treat ADHD are divided into short-acting medications, which need to be taken several times a day to maintain their effectiveness, and long-acting medications, which allow for greater time between doses. The success of long-acting stimulants has led the majority of physicians to prescribe them in preference to the short-acting variety.

Short-Acting Medications
- **Ritalin.** (The generic name is methylphenidate.) Ritalin is considered obsolete, although some physicians continue to use it because they are most familiar with it. In most cases, Ritalin has been replaced by Focalin. A typical dose of Ritalin ranges from 5 to 20 mg three times a day. Since each dose lasts only three to four hours, several doses are required each day.
- **Focalin.** (The generic name is dexmethylphenidate.) A typical dose ranges from 2.5 to 10 mg three times a day. It is basically the new and improved Ritalin, with a different chemical formula.
- **Dexedrine.** Dexedrine is no longer in general use for ADHD. A typical dose ranges from 5 to 20 mg twice a day.
- **Adderall.** A typical dose ranges from 5 to 20 mg twice a day. Since each dose only lasts four to five hours, several doses are required each day. It is composed of Dexedrine, sustained-release Dexedrine, and various salts. It is basically the new and improved Dexedrine. Adderall tends to last longer than Ritalin or Focalin. It is more potent than Ritalin: 5 mg of Adderall may be equivalent to about 7 mg of Ritalin. Recently, concerns about heart-related deaths and strokes in children and especially in adults have prompted Canada Health, a government agency, to call for the withdrawal of Adderall from the market. The FDA is also considering adding a warning, similar to that on SSRI antidepressants, on Adderall labels. Check with your physician about the latest information.

Long-Acting Medications
- **Concerta.** Concerta is currently the most commonly used stimulant medication to treat the symptoms of ADHD. This sustained-release stimulant medication is compared to Ritalin in the following chart:

CONCERTA	DOSAGE EQUIVALENT FOR RITALIN
18 mg once daily	5 mg three times a day
36 mg once daily	10 mg three times a day
54 mg once daily	15 mg three times a day

The pills cannot be crushed or split in half because of their sustained-release nature. Doing so would render them ineffective. While drug companies suggest that Concerta can last from nine to twelve hours, my experience, confirmed by many other mental health practitioners, is that it lasts only about nine hours.

- **Adderall XR.** The minimum dose for this sustained-release stimulant medication is 5 mg and can go up to 20 mg. Adderall XR is more potent than Concerta when comparing milligrams, but it generally doesn't last as long (eight hours). One advantage of Adderall XR is that it comes in a capsule form and can be used for children who can't swallow a pill.

- **Metadate CD.** This sustained-release stimulant medication, the equivalent of taking two doses of Ritalin a day, tends to last only six hours. Although it doesn't last as long as Concerta, it may have fewer side effects. Like Adderall XR, it also comes in a capsule form and can be used for children who can't swallow a pill. It comes in 10 mg doses. Taking 10 mg is like taking a 10 mg dose of Ritalin.

- **Ritalin LA.** Ritalin LA (long acting) is a sustained-release version of Ritalin that works more quickly than Concerta but may not last as long. It is similar to Metadate CD in that it is a six-hour medication. A common starting dose is 20 mg, and it comes in a capsule form. A 20 mg dose of Ritalin LA is like taking two 10 mg doses of short-acting Ritalin.

- **Strattera.** This new nonstimulant medication is used to treat ADHD. It appears to have beneficial effects but doesn't appear to be as effective as the stimulants in focusing attention. However, it has fewer side effects and often has a positive impact on children who haven't responded to stimulants. The dosage for children usually starts at 18 mg and increases over a period of days to an average of 60 mg. With older teenagers, the starting and ending doses may be higher (almost double).

- **Wellbutrin SR.** In addition to its use as an antidepressant, Wellbutrin has also been used to treat symptoms of ADHD, but its effect on attention span is only mild. Wellbutrin SR should be taken twice daily, unlike Wellbutrin XL, which is taken once a day.

The medications used to treat ADHD are considered safe when properly monitored. They don't damage any organs of the body, and there is no evidence that they cause any physical harm. However, if one has a heart defect, it may preclude the use of this type of medication. Monitoring the child's blood pressure is usually recommended, although high blood pressure is a relatively rare side effect. None of the children I've seen in my practice, for example, have had elevated blood pressure as a result of taking one of these medications.

The most common side effects of stimulant medication are loss of appetite and difficulty sleeping. If these problems persist over time, trial of another medication may be advisable. Other side effects might be mild physical discomfort in the form of headaches or stomachaches.

If a child becomes extremely agitated or extremely lethargic while taking stimulant medications, a parent should let the physician know immediately. These side effects indicate that the medication may need to be discontinued or adjusted. If motor tics, such as eye blinking or facial grimaces, develop, the physician should also be notified. While stimulant medications don't cause motor tics, they can promote a tendency to exhibit motor tics that already exist.

Anxiety

About half the children experiencing depression also experience anxiety.

As with depression, anxiety often has a genetic component. When I work with an anxious child, I often discover that someone else in the family exhibits a similar profile. Because a susceptibility to both depression and anxiety may be inherited, whenever I deal with a depressed child, I also look at symptoms of anxiety.

Anxiety is easy to overlook because a child may not talk about his fears, especially if he's an adolescent. Young children tend to be much more open and at ease in sharing their fears and worries.

Anxiety usually takes one of two forms: a generalized anxiety disorder or a more specific anxiety related to panic attacks. Symptoms of generalized anxiety relate to feelings of restlessness, being on edge, being overwhelmed, having difficulty concentrating, and experiencing muscle tension or sleep disturbance. With generalized anxiety, there may be more fears, but they aren't as intense as when a panic attack is involved.

The most common forms of a panic attack in children relate to school phobia or separation anxiety when a child is asked to leave the physical proximity of a parent. Children in these situations may become so anxious that they throw up, have major temper tantrums, and act defiant, even if they're usually well behaved.

The Differences Between Anxiety and Depression. Anxiety differs from depression in that an anxious child usually has more energy and doesn't have as much of a negative attitude toward life. Instead, the anxious child is afraid and has fears that impede her ability to meet the demands placed on her. Anxiety can have a negative impact on her ability to attend school, engage in social activities, and simply be able to relax.

While the anxious child may avoid participating in activities, she does so for a different reason than the depressed child. The anxious child tries to avoid dealing with situations that make her nervous. The depressed child avoids dealing with a situation because she lacks the energy and frustration tolerance to deal with it. The anxious child also experiences the stress of perceived negative events more intensely.

But there's one way in which anxiety and depression are similar. Threats regarding the negative consequences of a child's behavior almost never produce the desired results. Instead, they'll probably make the situation worse. Threatening an anxious child will only cause more anxiety and lead to an "Oh, no!" response. The depressed child may not react to the threat because she doesn't have the energy or motivation to care, which results in a "So what?" response.

Counseling and Medication for Anxiety. Anxiety and depression often require different treatments, both in counseling and in the use of medication. If a mental health professional focuses solely on the depression and ignores the anxiety, the child won't get adequate help to deal effectively with his fears and his resulting impairments.

The objective of treatment is to reduce the child's anxiety level. If a child's symptoms are mild, medication won't be needed and counseling alone usually provides good results. However, if a child's impairment is severe and significantly impacts her ability to perform ordinary life tasks, such as doing well at school and interacting with children and adults, and leads her to become increasingly dependent, medication can be a beneficial component of effective treatment. Just as with depression, what many professionals advocate is a combination of counseling and medication.

Phobias or panic attacks may be treated through either systematic desensitization or implosive therapy. With systematic desensitization, a therapist tries to ease a child into the stressful experience by developing a hierarchy of lower-level stressful situations and asking the child to imagine doing them before actually engaging in them. For example, a child might be asked to imagine getting dressed for school, getting on the bus or into a car, leaving the bus or car, entering the school, and going into the classroom. Then, with a parent's help, the child might practice doing these activities over the weekend, when school isn't in session. Finally, the child would practice doing them on a school day. Implosive therapy works on the assumption that if you are afraid of riding a motorcycle, you have to get on one and lose your fears. In this situation, a parent might take her child to school, leave the vicinity as soon as possible, and ask the school staff to deal with the problem. In most cases, the situation will be resolved, but in extreme cases, it may not. The effectiveness of these treatments will vary from child to child.

The medications used to treat anxiety are often the same ones used to treat depression. If the SSRIs (Prozac, Zoloft, Paxil, Celexa, Lexapro) don't work, a physician might try Effexor or BuSpar, a mild antianxiety medication. I am strongly against putting a child on an addictive antianxiety medication, such as Xanax or Valium—the long-term consequences of addiction and withdrawal are simply too negative for any benefit they might offer.

Obsessive-Compulsive Disorder

Obsessive-compulsive disorder (OCD) is a type of anxiety disorder that relates to the strong need to keep thinking about something or repeating the same type of behavior. These thoughts and behaviors are very disturbing to the child—she doesn't want them to be happening, and yet she can't seem to stop them. The thoughts are irrational and have no logic. For example, a child might have thoughts about bad things happening to a parent and simply cannot get them out of her mind. A compulsion is a behavior that is repeated, such as having to tap your toe on the threshold three times before you enter a house. Or it might involve compulsive washing or bathing. The compulsive child cannot feel comfortable until he has engaged in his own private ritual.

A child suffering from OCD often feels embarrassed by what she's doing and thinking. Many times, because this behavior may be private, a parent may not be aware of how severe the problem is. Sometimes it is only when a therapist sees a child alone in the counseling session that a report of the distressing thoughts or behaviors come to light.

Counseling and Medication for OCD. The first step in treating OCD is to have the child see a psychologist or other mental health professional who has had success in dealing with this disorder. Many different strategies might be used in counseling, depending on the child and his particular needs, and the more experience a counselor has with this disorder, the better.

One strategy I've used in counseling certain children might sound confusing to some parents, and indeed, it's paradoxical—but for some children, it is surprisingly effective. Working with the parents and the child, I ask the family to set up a schedule of times in which the child has to practice exhibiting the compulsive behavior or thinking about the obsession. I usually ask the child to do this for five or ten minutes while the parent times her. When the time is up, the child is to think about a time she felt good or happy. If she can't think of one, she is to make up one. This strategy usually shows results within a week, if it's going to work at all. Doing this exercise gives a child an opportunity to have some control over the anxiety by turning it on and off. It is the practice of turning it off that is particularly beneficial, since the child will learn to generalize this practice and use it in her real-world experiences.

Another strategy that I've used in relation to hand or body movements is to have the child practice them in front of a mirror for several minutes a day, to become more aware of his actions. I find that the increased awareness helps the child know what he needs to change.

If these strategies or other counseling approaches are ineffective, another possible treatment to explore is the use of an SSRI antidepressant, such as Zoloft, Paxil, Celexa, Lexapro, or Prozac. At relatively higher doses, these medications tend to be effective in treating obsessive or compulsive behaviors. I have also seen success with the use of Effexor to treat OCD symptoms. These medications may help treat the OCD by lowering the child's anxiety and overall stress level, which fits with the notion that OCD can be thought of as a subtype of anxiety disorder.

Substance Abuse

A child who has a substance abuse problem with alcohol, marijuana, or other illegal drugs presents a unique challenge in treating depression. In my practice, I've found that a child with a substance abuse problem often has little motivation to participate in treatment for mental health issues. He gets high, which leads him to feel (falsely) that he doesn't have any problems, and then he decides that it's his parents and teachers who have the problems. He doesn't care if he doesn't complete his schoolwork, follow household rules, or do chores at home. He doesn't want to be bothered and just wants to be left alone.

However, when a child isn't functioning well, it's especially hard for a parent to leave her child alone. Often, parents have a sense that the substance abuse is a way that a child is seeking something that is missing in her life. In many cases, the alcohol or the drugs are the only way a child has found to dull the pain, confusion, or anxiety she's feeling, which is why such behavior is sometimes referred to as self-medication—except that people who turn to this solution are not only *not* helping themselves deal with their problems, they are actively making their problems worse.

Use or Abuse? There are different levels of substance usage. While most people prefer that their child not engage in any drinking or drug use, it's important to recognize the difference between a child who smokes marijuana twice a month versus one who does it every day or even several times a week. A child who drinks alone or smokes marijuana by herself is probably trying to self-medicate, and until she gives up the substance abuse, it's less likely that she'll effectively participate in treatment. Her use of these substances allows her to avoid dealing with the issues causing her pain, creating a cycle of avoidance and failure and more avoidance. She might even carry over that avoidance when it comes to counseling.

The following guidelines might help you determine the nature and the seriousness of your child's substance abuse:

- Does she use the substance at home?
- Is he selling video games or CDs to come up with money (presumably to buy drugs)?
- Has she developed a stealing problem recently?
- Do most of his friends abuse alcohol or drugs?
- Are you unaware of where she is most evenings?
- Does he frequently have bloodshot eyes for no medical reason?
- Are you missing bottles of alcohol at your home?
- Does she go outside the house for brief periods of time at night for no apparent reason?
- Has he been caught using drugs or alcohol?
- Does she talk a lot about marijuana to others?

Parents may seek help, but counseling often is ineffective because the child has become addicted, whether physically or emotionally or both, to drugs or alcohol and isn't ready to change—or may not know how to change on her own.

Some programs that may be of help in addressing alcohol and drug abuse include Alcoholics Anonymous and Narcotics Anonymous, each of which may have special meetings for teens in your area.

If the addiction becomes severe, a child may need inpatient treatment at a hospital that deals with substance abuse issues in order to get better.

Having a substance abuse problem also complicates a child's treatment because of the negative effect the illegal drugs or alcohol can have with prescription medications. Most physicians simply won't prescribe antidepressant medications to a person who has an alcohol abuse problem. When someone combines antidepressant medication with one or two drinks, the level of intoxication may be magnified and could even be fatal if the person who combines alcohol and anti-depressants gets behind the wheel of a car.

The risk of suicide also increases when a depressed person uses alcohol or drugs, because inhibitions may be lowered, and a child who otherwise wouldn't carry through on a suicide attempt might do so when he has had a couple of drinks.

Sometimes doctors and therapists have to be a little like detectives and have to keep hunting for the clues and the evidence that will lead them to the right answer. As we've seen, sometimes there are several answers—several mental health issues that must be addressed in order for a child to get better.

A Plan for Parents

▶ Don't assume that just because your child has symptoms of depression she can't have another mental
  health condition.
▶ Make sure that your child has been assessed for other
  mental health conditions in order to rule them in or
  rule them out.
▶ Focus on your child's impairments and not on a label.
▶ Make sure that your child is properly diagnosed. An
  incorrect or incomplete diagnosis can lead to the
  wrong treatment or prevent you from accessing strategies that would lead to more success.

7

Depression and Bipolar Disorder

I'VE DEVOTED A separate chapter to bipolar disorder because it is a mood disorder directly related to depression, and as you'll see, the treatment for one can be inappropriate for the other. Please read this chapter carefully, since a child experiencing bipolar disorder presents great challenges to his family and to the treating mental health professionals. Early identification and treatment are critical to getting positive results.

Bipolar disorder used to be called manic depressive disorder, which implies mood swings from mania to depression. Until about 2000, a diagnosis of bipolar disorder in a child was relatively rare. The common view was that nobody experienced bipolar disorder prior to adolescence. This is the same kind of thinking that previously existed regarding childhood depression and has since been shown to be wrong. Followers of psychoanalytic theory especially used to believe that children couldn't become depressed or have manic depression. Current psychology has a very different view. Children can and do become depressed. Children can and do suffer from bipolar disorder.

While both bipolar disorder and depression are mood disorders, the former is more incapacitating because it has a greater negative effect on a child's current and long-term functioning. Bipolar disorder is less common than depression, but it is more chronic and debilitating. Everyone has changes in mood over time, but those ordinary changes aren't as intense as they are in someone who is diagnosed with bipolar disorder.

Children who have had an episode of depression appear to be at higher risk of developing bipolar disorder as they get older, as compared to children who never experienced depression. At least 20 to 30 percent of children with depression will eventually experience bipolar disorder.

Symptoms of Bipolar Disorder

Like many other mental health disorders, bipolar disorder appears to be a highly inheritable condition. If a child has bipolar disorder, the probability is greater than 30 percent that one of his parents also meets the criteria for diagnosis.

Children often manifest bipolar disorder differently than adults, exhibiting less clearly defined ups and downs. Instead of prolonged periods of depression and mania, children demonstrate chronic cycling and irritability. A child's moods are likely to be up one minute, down the next, and then sideways after that—a very unstable situation, indeed. In a child, the manic cycle is less clearly defined than is the depressive cycle.

Another difference is that adults tend to be more articulate in expressing their moods than children are. Because adults verbalize both their mania and depressive symptoms, it may be easier for family members to identify their ups and downs. With children, the mood swings are identified primarily by the changes in the child's behavior.

The symptoms of bipolar disorder often start out looking like a depression and later transform into manic (intensely agitated) behavior.

- **Being depressed.** One of the significant elements of a bipolar disorder diagnosis is an underlying depression. In some sense, bipolar disorder is depression with the added symptoms associated with mania or extreme irritability. With bipolar disorder, the symptoms of depression are often more intense; a child may spend considerable time talking about death and dying, for example.

- **Irritable or angry mood.** Everyday irritability comes and goes and usually has a visible trigger, but bipolar irritability is more like chronic and intense grumpiness that impacts all areas of a child's functioning. The anger and chronic upset are more intense, and the child's responses are way out of proportion, given the situation.
- **Periods of being overly silly, impulsive, and active.** Some misinformed people might confuse these symptoms with ADHD. The major difference is that these symptoms haven't always been present, as they are with ADHD. Instead, they arise fairly suddenly and then may disappear. These moods can be intense. Parents, frustrated at their inability to have any impact on their child's behavior during these moods, find them difficult to handle. Parents also may have difficulty communicating with their child when she's impulsive and excessively active.
- **Increased violence.** A child with bipolar disorder tends to be more violent and hits, kicks, bites, breaks, or throws objects at others. He has difficulty handling the intense irritability he is experiencing and reacts with more extreme emotions than the average depressed child.
- **Grandiosity.** Children and adults with bipolar disorder often have exaggerated opinions of their capabilities. They may talk about how they're the best at something, when in fact their skills are relatively average. They might even make comments that other children are incapable of measuring up to their talents and abilities.
- **Sleep difficulties.** Sometimes children with bipolar disorder stay up all night, engaging in a variety of activities, moving restlessly from one to the next. They are so energized that they can't go to sleep. After a time, they pay a price for the lack of sleep and become even more depressed and fatigued.

Some children with bipolar disorder may have an unhealthy obsession with sex, drugs, or alcohol. Occasionally, children with bipolar disorder experience auditory or visual hallucinations. This isn't common, but I have seen it happen on several occasions. These children don't meet the other criteria for schizophrenia, in which the hallucinations and delusions are more intense and pervasive, last longer, and don't usually go away on their own.

Diagnosing Bipolar Disorder

Diagnosing bipolar disorder in a child is a difficult process. Because professionals have only recently agreed that this disorder can occur in children, we don't yet have formal, concrete, and universally accepted criteria for such a diagnosis. Any diagnosis of bipolar disorder in a child should be confirmed by a child psychiatrist. To make matters even more complicated, a child may have bipolar disorder and other conditions (such as ADHD, conduct disorder, oppositional defiant disorder, OCD, or anxiety disorder) at the same time.

When considering a diagnosis of bipolar disorder, the family history is often a big help to me. When other members of a child's family have been previously diagnosed with a mental health issue, it serves as a pointer to investigate the possibility that the child is manifesting an inherited problem. A family history of alcohol or drug abuse can also be a red flag for diagnosing bipolar disorder. While most people with substance abuse don't have bipolar disorder, some research suggests that approximately half the adults with bipolar disorder have a substance abuse problem. My theory is that these adults are trying to self-medicate because of the inability to tolerate their symptoms.

The symptoms of bipolar disorder and other mental health conditions can be hard to differentiate. However, it's critical that this differential diagnosis be made, since the medications used to treat depression, ADHD, or anxiety may make the symptoms of bipolar disorder worse. The medication doesn't cause bipolar disorder, but if a child who is undiagnosed is given an antidepressant, the onset of symptoms may be accelerated.

I need to say this again, because it's so important: *the medications used to treat depression, ADHD, or anxiety may make the symptoms of bipolar disorder worse.*

The use of an antidepressant may fuel a child's mania, making her more agitated, restless, and even violent. Sometimes the SSRI antidepressants, like Prozac, Zoloft, or Paxil, can accelerate the process of a depressed child becoming manic. For reasons not completely understood, Wellbutrin appears least likely to move a child from an ordinary depression into bipolar disorder. That doesn't mean it should be the first choice for all children, however—many other factors are part of that decision, as we've already seen.

If you suspect that your child is at risk for bipolar disorder, you need to be especially conservative in the use of antidepressant medication. You should be extra cautious about your child going on higher doses of medication. Your child's medications should be closely monitored by a child psychiatrist who has training and experience in dealing with the special problems presented by this condition.

▶ **Antidepressants and the Onset of Bipolar Disorder**

Becky is a nine-year-old child whose use of antidepressant medication led to the onset of bipolar disorder. She came to see me because she was experiencing significant, severe symptoms of depression, and she spoke about killing herself. No major event or stress in her life seemed to explain the intensity of her feelings. When I did a family history with her parents, they mentioned that there was a history of depression on her mother's side of the family, although neither parent reported symptoms of mental health problems. During counseling, Becky often cried, but she had great difficulty saying what was making her so unhappy.

After my first session with Becky, I contacted her pediatrician to discuss placing her on an antidepressant to alleviate her severe symptoms. She was started on 25 mg of Zoloft. In two weeks, her depression lifted. I saw her smile for the first time, and we had few problems to talk about in the counseling session because she was happy. She was doing well in school, and everything appeared to be all right.

Two months later, her parents contacted me again to say that Becky had become aggressive and hyperactive. Her school behavior had deteriorated, and it was difficult for her parents to control her. I told her parents to bring her in that night, and when she stepped into my office, I saw what they were talking about. She couldn't sit still but rather jiggled her foot and tapped her fingers, getting up and walking around periodically, and she couldn't focus long enough to participate in a simple conversation. I called her pediatrician the next day, and it was decided to wean her off the Zoloft.

Even after the Zoloft was discontinued, however, Becky continued to be aggressive and hyperactive. I suspected that she might have bipolar disorder, and I again asked her parents if anyone in the family had similar symptoms. After they had time to think about it, they mentioned that her maternal grandmother had similar symptoms and was in fact diagnosed with manic depression (the old term for bipolar disorder). This was important information that would have been helpful during the initial diagnosis.

I recommended that Becky's parents take her to a child psychiatrist to be evaluated for bipolar disorder. Her parents ended up going to a psychiatrist with whom I wasn't familiar. He diagnosed her as having ADHD, at least in part because the school had filled out forms suggesting that she was exhibiting symptoms of ADHD. I talked to her school psychologist, who also had come to the conclusion that Becky had ADHD.

However, to my way of thinking, the onset of the symptoms was all wrong. She had never exhibited hyperactive behavior prior to the age of nine, and there was no family history of similar symptoms. I shared my concerns with her psychiatrist, who still insisted that Becky had ADHD and proceeded to prescribe Concerta to treat her hyperactivity and impulsivity. When she began to take Concerta, Becky immediately became worse, exhibiting greater irritability and more violence. In the meantime, Becky's parents had made an appointment with another psychiatrist, one I'd recommended, to get a second opinion. This psychiatrist agreed with my diagnosis of bipolar disorder and prescribed Depakote, which led to a significant improvement within two weeks. Becky's hyperactivity went away, and she was able to listen to her parents and her teachers. She no longer exhibited signs of depression.

Becky continues to do well, and her mood, activity level, and compliance are now in the normal range for a child of her age.

As Becky's story shows, mental health professionals can make mistakes. A diagnosis is dependent on the data that the mental health professional receives, and interpretations can be subjective. Parents need to keep in mind that just because a child exhibits some symptoms of a disorder, she doesn't necessarily have that disability. Often, knowing when a problem started can be the key factor in reaching an accurate diagnosis.

Treatment of Bipolar Disorder

Bipolar disorder is more difficult to treat than typical depression. Multiple medications may be involved, they often take longer to be effective, and they may be less effective. A child with bipolar disorder also presents more behavioral difficulties and will likely be harder for parents to deal with because of the frequent mood changes. Just as with depression, the child is likely to benefit from a combination of counseling and medication.

It's important for parents to remember that a child with bipolar disorder has an illness that causes him to misbehave. Don't label your child a juvenile delinquent and get into battles over his severe behavior problems. Most children don't want to misbehave, and they take no pleasure in getting into trouble. When you see a child with bipolar disorder having difficulty controlling his outbursts, keep in mind that he's not exploding on purpose. If a child has bipolar disorder, the whole family may benefit from counseling, since the child's disability will have an impact on everyone. Just being aware of the true nature of the problem and what's being done to try to improve the situation may help siblings be more understanding about what's happening within the family.

In general, the counseling procedures used for depression also apply to bipolar disorder. The major difference is that bipolar disorder involves more symptoms and potentially aggressive behaviors that are more difficult to treat.

Medications

The medications used to treat bipolar disorder can take a long time to become effective and have the potential for many side effects. They should be administered through the supervision of a trained child psychiatrist, because the child's blood levels need to be carefully monitored. For some children with this illness, a combination of medications may be necessary, and that demands expert monitoring.

- **Mood stabilizers.** Lithium is probably the most widely known mood stabilizer. It has a long history of use for treatment of bipolar disorder and is generally a very effective medication. However, lithium can be toxic to the kidneys, so physicians are required to do periodic blood work to monitor kidney function and levels of lithium in the blood.

  Lamictal is a newer mood stabilizer that isn't toxic to the kidneys but may not be as effective as lithium. Skin rashes, one of the side effects of this medication, should be immediately reported to a physician.

- **Anticonvulsants.** Anticonvulsants are medications used to treat seizure disorders. However, researchers have found that they can also be effective in stabilizing mood disorders. Depakote is one of these medications that has been demonstrated to be effective in stabilizing the moods of people experiencing bipolar disorder.

  In my experience, Depakote has been the first choice of most psychiatrists treating children experiencing symptoms of bipolar disorder. It can take two to three weeks to see benefits from the medication, and the full effect may not be seen for six to eight weeks. Depakote should be prescribed by a child psychiatrist who is familiar with how children react to it. It has more potential side effects than the typical antidepressant and therefore needs good monitoring by someone with expertise in prescribing it. Because it is potentially toxic to the liver, the physician needs to do periodic blood work. Other side effects that should be reported are fatigue, stomach discomfort, possible weight gain, and vomiting.

  Topamax and Neurontin are also anticonvulsants that have been used to treat bipolar disorder. They tend to be less effective than Depakote but also have fewer side effects. Children on these medications are less likely to experience weight gain or liver toxicity.

  Tegretol has also been used to treat bipolar disorder but has been used primarily with adults. Tegretol may be used with children when Depakote hasn't been effective. Tegretol has many of the same potential side effects as Depakote and can also affect a child's red blood cell count. Recently, a milder version of Tegretol, called Trileptal, came out. While it may potentially be less effective than Tegretol, it appears to be safer and has fewer side effects.

- **Antipsychotics.** Respirdal, Zyprexa, Seroquel, Abilify, and Geodon are used to treat psychotic disorders and don't have the significant side effects that were observed with the previous generation of these drugs, such as Haldol or Mellaril. When a mood stabilizer or an anticonvulsant isn't sufficient to treat a child's symptoms, an antipsychotic may need to be introduced. These medications can be an effective addition to the treatment regimen, even though a child isn't exhibiting any psychotic-like symptoms. The antipsychotic medications are often helpful in treating a child's aggressive, manic behavior, but it may take several weeks to determine their effectiveness.

If your child is taking any of these medications, it's important that you monitor her for fatigue, hand or leg shaking, and weight gain, especially if she's taking Zyprexa. Limiting food portions, following a careful diet, and getting exercise are important for children taking these types of medications. Again, the physician usually does periodic blood work for children on these medications to monitor their effectiveness and to check kidney or liver functions.

Hospitalization

A child with bipolar disorder is at higher risk for needing hospitalization than a child with depression. Her symptoms are more intense, and the heightened irritability plus impulsivity can raise safety issues. If you or a psychiatrist or mental health professional believes that your child's safety may be at risk, it's important to have your child assessed for hospitalization.

If hospitalization is recommended for your child, you need to be aware of a couple of very important things. First, bipolar disorder is complicated and isn't easy to diagnose, so it is often misdiagnosed or missed altogether by health professionals.

I cannot repeat often enough how critical it is for your therapist to talk to the hospital staff, particularly the staff psychiatrist who is treating a child. Your child's therapist has a great deal of knowledge and insight regarding his condition, especially if counseling has been ongoing for several months. As an example of how critical this communication is, I offer the story of Ben.

▶ **The Importance of Making an Accurate Diagnosis**

Ben was a ten-year-old boy who initially lived with his mother and stepfather and then went to live with his father and stepmother after his mother died. His parents had divorced when he was two, and they'd had a rocky relationship even after the divorce. His mother, Ginny, had a substance abuse problem and was depressed, and she was reported to have had frequent mood swings. She was abusive to Ben and often hit him and called him names. One day when Ben was out of the house, she took an overdose of pills and died.

Until Ginny died, Ben's father, Joel, who lived in a different state, had infrequent contact with Ben. When he went to live with his father, Ben was difficult to manage and refused to listen to parental requests. He was physically violent and threw objects at his father and stepmother with all his might. He also kicked and punched them when they didn't give him what he wanted. Ben's behavior was so out of control that the issue of hospitalization was discussed in my office.

I wanted to avoid hospitalizing him, if that was possible. Ben had lost his mother recently and was just beginning to establish a relationship with his father. But Joel and his wife felt overwhelmed and didn't know how to manage Ben.

I knew that Ben was angry and upset, but I didn't have enough information to provide a clear diagnosis, since his behavior could have been a reaction to the stress he'd experienced in his young life. An abused child who loses a parent and moves to a new state to establish a relationship with his father is clearly overwhelmed—Ben's stress load was enormous. I felt that he was in a crisis situation and consulted with his pediatrician regarding medication that might help curb his violence.

Ideally, I would have liked him to be seen by a child psychiatrist, but it would have taken at least six weeks to get him an appointment. His physician placed him on Wellbutrin SR and later added a 1 mg dose of Tenex, an antihypertension drug that in small doses helps to lower activity level and aggressive behavior. This treatment seemed to make a huge difference in Ben's irritability and violent behavior. After ten days, he looked like a completely different child. He began to listen to his parents and was no longer violent. He still had a bad temper, but it was under control.

I continued to see Ben and his parents approximately every other week for several months and was pleased with his progress. He was doing well in school and was making friends, and his behavior was manageable at home. He still had difficulty listening to his stepmother, but things were improving. However, things began to change about a year after our first visit. Ben began to withdraw from his friends and engage in strange behaviors. He put shaving cream on his face and shaved off his eyebrows, he went outside his window to climb on the roof in the middle of the night, and he took an overdose of his Wellbutrin. He was also angrier and was becoming violent again.

When Ben was upset, he opened his window and threw objects out of the house. His father had to bolt the window shut because he was concerned for Ben's safety—and for the safety of anyone who might be passing by.

I believed that Ben was exhibiting symptoms of bipolar disorder and shared my impression with his parents. I suggested that his parents take Ben to the local hospital to be evaluated for placement because I was concerned for his safety. Again, I would have liked him to see a child psychiatrist on an emergency basis, but this couldn't be accomplished.

Ben was evaluated by a local psychiatric hospital with an excellent reputation, and it was agreed that he needed to be placed. Since a bed was not available for him at this hospital, he had to go to another hospital, in a nearby town. I called the hospital to speak to his treating psychiatrist and left several phone numbers, including my office, service, and home numbers. The psychiatrist never called me. Ben's caseworker left a message on my voice mail six days after he was admitted, saying that Ben was being discharged and he wanted to make sure that I'd schedule a follow-up appointment. When I returned his call, Ben's psychiatrist happened to be in the office.

She apologized for not getting back to me and told me that she had diagnosed Ben with posttraumatic stress disorder and was prescribing Lexapro to treat his anxiety and improve his mood. Lexapro, an antidepressant in the SSRI family, may bring on episodes of mania in bipolar individuals. When I told her that I was concerned because I felt that Ben was exhibiting symptoms of bipolar disorder, she replied that she had already made her diagnosis (which was done without my input) and had ruled out bipolar disorder. I was taken aback by her dismissal of the value of listening to a child's treating therapist before reaching her conclusion. She made sure to say, "I wouldn't prescribe Lexapro if I thought Ben had bipolar disorder."

I was deeply concerned that Ben wasn't getting adequate treatment. The problems that had put him in the hospital weren't being addressed, and his treatment had the potential to make things considerably worse for him. I played telephone tag with Ben's parents for several days and finally gave them my home phone number. I almost never do that, but I was so concerned about Ben that I felt it was necessary.

His parents told me that Ben was back in the local hospital because his behavior had severely deteriorated. He was hallucinating, had become violent, and was extremely agitated. During a car ride, he tried to get out of the car at a major intersection and walk into traffic. Eventually, Ben was placed in another psychiatric hospital and was diagnosed with bipolar disorder and released after a stay of a month. He was prescribed Depakote to stabilize his mood but couldn't tolerate it because of stomach discomfort. Eventually, he was prescribed several medications that have needed constant adjustment. He is currently taking lithium, Seroquel, and Zyprexa. He still has his ups and downs, and we are continuing to work on making progress. My main goal in the counseling has been to keep up the hope that things will get better.

I'm not perfect. I don't claim to have all the answers all the time. But a therapist who has had an ongoing relationship with a child is likely to have valuable insights that should be shared with a hospital's therapist and psychiatrist. Doctors do make mistakes sometimes. Parents of a child who is hospitalized should insist that the child's therapist talk to the hospital's therapist and psychiatrist so they don't have to suffer the same distress Ben and his family were subjected to.

Long-Term Residential Placement

Children with bipolar disorder are at increased risk for long-term placement in a psychiatric or medical facility outside of their home. The severe intensity of their emotions places them at risk for engaging in unsafe behavior that could lead to hospitalization and, eventually, residential placement. No parent wants to see her child placed outside the family home. Residential treatment isn't done primarily with the idea of providing better and more effective treatment for a child—it is a traumatic experience and should be avoided, if possible. However, when your child's safety, your safety, or the safety of your other children is endangered, this may be the only viable option.

The safety of the people in your family must come first. Only then can other concerns be addressed. Consider Brett's story.

▶ Protecting the Safety of All Family Members

Brett was seven years old and had severe symptoms of bipolar disorder. He was referred to my private practice by his pediatrician because of severely aggressive and uncontrollable behavior at home. He became violent when he was upset and punched holes in walls and broke objects, especially things his parents liked. He had even broken his parents' car window twice when he threw objects in anger.

Brett lived with his mother, Liz, his father, Eugene, and two younger sisters. His oldest sister had been diagnosed with bipolar disorder when she was sixteen and was temporarily placed out of her home by the local Department of Social Services because her parents couldn't control her.

Brett's mother was often sad, was sometimes agitated, and had a problem with alcohol abuse. Liz never sought treatment for the drinking or her mood swings, which I suspected were symptoms of undiagnosed bipolar disorder. Eugene was an anxious person who tended to be physically active and spoke about his worries about being able to control his children. He'd taken Xanax to treat his anxiety for a brief time.

I saw Brett for approximately four years. Hyperactive and impulsive, he initially presented symptoms suggestive of ADHD. He had great difficulty completing his work in school. In looking at the family history, I recognized that many variables could have caused these symptoms. While he met the criteria for a diagnosis of ADHD, his symptoms might also be explained by anxiety or bipolar disorder. I therefore recommended that his parents take him to a child psychiatrist to get another opinion.

The psychiatrist diagnosed him with ADHD and prescribed Ritalin. Brett had a good response and seemed to be more under control. He started to do a little better in school and was less violent. However, this progress didn't last long, and he began to regress in about six weeks. The psychiatrist then increased his medication, and a similar pattern occurred. Brett briefly responded to a change in medication, but after a short time, it had little effect or even made him worse. In Brett's case, his appetite diminished and the intensity of his anger increased. I communicated this to the psychiatrist, and Brett was eventually placed on Respirdal, an antipsychotic medication often used as a mood stabilizer. Again a brief positive result came—and then went away. Now, instead of losing weight, Brett gained about forty pounds and was in danger of becoming obese. The psychiatrist tried other mood stabilizers, such as Neurontin. He added Zoloft as an antidepressant, but Brett showed no change in his functioning.

Everyone involved—the psychiatrist, Liz and Eugene, Brett, and I— were really frustrated. Eventually, Brett's parents took him to another psychiatrist, and he once again showed a pattern of brief positive response and then regression to previous performance. He was placed on two antidepressants (Prozac and Paxil) and on an anticonvulsant medication (Depakote) without showing any progress.

Brett ended up being hospitalized on two occasions over the years because his behavior had become unsafe to himself and to his family. He hit his sisters with all his strength and left bruises on several family members. He once threw a heavy ashtray at his father's head, just missing him. What concerned me most was a report that Brett had begun threatening family members with a steak knife whenever he was upset.

I'd love to be able to tell you that Brett's symptoms became better and that he no longer needs treatment. Unfortunately, bipolar disorder can be a very difficult condition to treat. When a child's symptoms don't respond to treatment, it can be extremely frustrating. His parents developed serious marital difficulties and a tolerance for misbehavior that I found to be alarming. Brett had thrown rocks at one of his sisters out of anger and opened a nasty wound on her head and had broken the arm of another sister. His parents had become desensitized to his unsafe behavior because it wasn't possible to react to every bad thing that he did. I felt that my counseling wasn't going to provide a cure for Brett, and my goal shifted to wanting to prevent escalation and keep the situation safe.

When the situation did become unsafe, I recommended that Brett be hospitalized. I believe that his parents will have to face the difficult dilemma of his having to go to a residential treatment facility eventually. By tolerating his unsafe behavior, Liz and Eugene were putting themselves and their daughters at risk. When dealing with families, ensuring a safe environment is my first concern. When a safe situation doesn't exist, hospitalization or a residential treatment facility should be explored.

Bipolar disorder is a serious problem, one of the most difficult mental health conditions to successfully treat. The high relapse rate indicates that mood swings may be a problem that your child will deal with for the rest of his life. If your child is diagnosed with bipolar disorder, he'll need continual monitoring by both a psychologist and a psychiatrist. Even if your child is feeling well and seems to be stabilized, you should still schedule periodic visits with a mental health professional at least once every few months. With proper treatment and monitoring, most children with bipolar disorder can lead a healthy and normal life.

A Plan for Parents

▶ If you suspect that your child has symptoms of bipolar disorder, arrange for an evaluation with a child psychiatrist who comes highly recommended by someone you trust.

▶ Request a second opinion from another doctor who is highly recommended if you have concerns about a diagnosis that was made regarding your child.

▶ See your child as having an unwanted disability and not as being defiant or bad.

▶ Don't focus on all the negative things that happen. Try to pick out one positive thing that your child does each day.

▶ Having a child with depression or bipolar disorder can create tension in a relationship. Work together with your partner and support each other.

▶ Look on the Internet for a support group for parents of children with bipolar disorder.

▶ Make use of an extended support group. You may need someone to watch your child so that you can take a breather.

▶ Keep reading the most current information about depression and bipolar disorder.

PART III

▼

The Journey Begins
Parenting the
Depressed Child

- ▶ How does depression affect school performance?
- ▶ What support services do schools provide?
- ▶ How does living with a depressed child affect the other children in my family?
- ▶ What are the benefits of routines for sleep, homework, and exercise?
- ▶ How can I help my child cultivate better peer relationships?
- ▶ How can I resolve conflicts and discipline a child who doesn't seem to care about anything?
- ▶ What is active listening?
- ▶ What can I do to help my child sustain improvements made during treatment?
- ▶ How can we set goals when we don't agree?

8

The School as Partner

▶   When Adam was fourteen, he was referred to me because his parents had asked for a learning disability evaluation. Adam's parents knew he was a bright child, and they couldn't understand why he was failing in school. He rarely completed his homework or studied for tests. His parents wanted to make sure that he didn't have a learning problem that was going undetected and therefore untreated. They had no idea that he was actually depressed.

When I began my assessment, I tried to be thorough and make sure that I didn't miss anything that might have impacted his school performance. I asked Adam and his parents to complete an ADHD rating scale. His parents reported significant concerns about his ability to focus but had little to say about hyperactivity or impulsivity. That told me that I should assess his ability to focus on tasks, and I gave him the Wide Range Assessment of Memory and Learning (WRAML). The test revealed that he did indeed have significant difficulty sustaining attention on the information he heard and saw. Adam also confirmed to me that he had difficulty concentrating.

The intelligence test I administered showed that he had an above average IQ of 120. I also administered tests that measured his ability to read, write, and work with numbers, and I determined that he had no impairments in his ability to learn. His reading and writing skills were above average, and his math skills were in the high average range.

I might have concluded that his focus difficulties were the result of ADHD-predominantly inattentive type. However, his early school records and his parents' anecdotal reports indicated that Adam's attention difficulties didn't start until middle school. If he truly had ADHD, the symptoms would have been present in his earlier years.

I suspected that Adam's school problems might be the result of depression, so I gave him the Beck Depression Inventory. He scored at the very high end of the depression scale. When it came time to discuss his responses, Adam told me that he'd been very unhappy for years, that he'd never gotten over his parents' divorce, and that he thought about killing himself almost every day. He hadn't acted on these thoughts because he felt a dim glimmer of hope, but it seemed to be fading.

His parents, who had focused on his school performance, had no clue about the depth of Adam's depression. They had no idea that he never got a good night's sleep and was always tired. He couldn't succeed in school at least in part because he didn't have the energy needed to complete his assignments.

Because of the severity of his symptoms, I called Adam's physician to discuss starting him on medication such as Lexapro, an antidepressant that works relatively quickly. Adam responded well to the treatment, including regular counseling sessions. He began to sleep better at night, and his mood improved. During counseling, we discussed the issues surrounding his parents' split-up, and slowly Adam learned to deal more effectively with the reality of their divorce.

I also contacted his guidance counselor to inform her that Adam was depressed and recommended she put together a parent-teacher-student meeting to review his school situation and develop a plan for improving his academic performance. During the meeting, Adam's math teacher volunteered that he had also experienced depression and that since being on medication he felt much better. Adam felt more comfortable knowing that his math teacher was also taking medication for depression. His teachers developed more sympathy and understanding for Adam, since they understood why he was doing poorly in school. At the meeting, it was agreed that Adam would see the school social worker once a week as part of a monitoring process to help him with any school problems. Adam also agreed to stay after school twice a week to work with his math and English teachers so that he could catch up on work he'd missed. Weekly progress reports were instituted, to keep his parents more closely informed of his progress in school.

Within a month, Adam's performance in school had dramatically improved. But even more important, his symptoms of depression had significantly declined and he no longer thought about killing himself.

How Depression Affects School Performance

When a child is failing or doing poorly in school, parents may react with understandable frustration and try all sorts of strategies, from bribery to punishment, to get their child to turn things around. When all things fail, tension rises and everyone becomes exasperated and at a loss to figure out the cause—and a cure—of the problems at school.

Depression, and not willfulness or laziness, might be at the bottom of things. Approximately 4 to 12 percent of school-aged children (depending upon their age) meet the criteria for being depressed, and since depression isn't just experienced at home, it's likely to affect a child's performance at school, too. Children experiencing symptoms of depression usually have difficulty completing schoolwork and are at risk for academic underachievement and failure. Without early diagnosis and treatment, a child is likely to be engaged in a negative cycle of depression ➤ school failure ➤ increased depression because of the failure.

School failure also has a negative impact on a child's self-esteem. A depressed child is apt to have difficulty working to her academic and intellectual capability. She seldom completes her homework, and her test grades are likely to go down because she is tired and has trouble concentrating. To complicate matters, her teachers may not recognize the symptoms of depression.

School may also be a source of stress for your child. For a depressed child, school may be the primary situation in which substantial demands are placed on her. Significant social stress might result if your child has difficulty fitting in with her peer group.

Parents and school staff need to work together to help a child move out of depression. Without shared information, it's impossible to come up with a coordinated plan. When parents and teachers don't understand a child's problems, it's hard for anyone to know how to help. If a child is diagnosed with depression, his teachers are more likely to have an increased sensitivity to his problems. I've participated in countless parent-teacher meetings in which a teacher mentions that she or some member of her family has also experienced depression. I'm always a bit relieved when this happens because that teacher is likely to have special sensitivity and understanding of the needs and stresses a depressed child experiences. Without an "official" diagnosis, your child might be perceived as being just another misbehaving kid who needs to be punished to learn that his actions have consequences. But this is futile for the depressed child—punishment usually results in more depression and doesn't lead to an improvement in functioning.

Depression is likely to affect your child in the following areas in school:

- **Ability to focus and pay attention.** The depressed child is often preoccupied with negative thoughts and feelings and finds it hard to put her full attention on schoolwork. Problems with concentration at school are one of the major complaints for children experiencing depression. A depressed child can improve her ability to sustain attention if she gets a good night's sleep and feels rested. I know that I have problems focusing when I haven't slept well, but it's even more difficult for the depressed child to overcome a lack of restful sleep.
- **Completing classwork.** When a child is depressed, he has little energy to apply to activities that he perceives as being stressful or of low interest. A depressed child may withdraw from typical activities and become resistant to teacher requests to participate in classroom activities. I've found it helpful to develop a behavior plan in which a child can gain privileges or concrete rewards for improving work production. In these situations, I ask that the teacher(s) provide daily feedback to parents regarding a child's completion of assignments. It works best if this is used in a positive instead of a negative way, so that it doesn't add undue pressure to the child's stress level. If he has a bad day, you can ignore it and try to focus on the next day being a better one.

- **Completing homework.** Children who are depressed often have great difficulty finishing their homework because they lack focus, energy, and motivation. Think about a depressed child as a battery low on power. It takes energy to complete an activity that isn't high on your interest level. Most children, of course, prefer to have no homework, but they do it because they know they have to. They're also aware that if they don't get it done, they may pay a price in the future. The depressed child is stuck in an unpleasant here and now. She's not thinking about the future, and when she does, it's without much hope or interest.

  You can try to improve homework production by working with your child to establish a regular routine for a time when there are few distractions, such as half an hour after coming home from school or after dinner. You might also create a behavior plan to set up rewards for good homework completion. If homework continues to be a problem, you can try to enroll your child in an after-school homework program or suggest finding a peer study buddy.

- **Getting to school.** Many depressed children have difficulty getting up in the morning and going to school. Because they are tired and have a hard time dealing with stressful events, they may try to avoid school altogether. You can help by encouraging your child to develop good routines for going to bed and waking up. The less your child has to think about what he has to do in the morning or at night, the better. The process should become automatic, so that it goes smoothly. Regular times for getting to bed and the use of a good alarm clock will also be helpful.

- **Peer relations.** Depressed children often have difficulties that lead to social isolation. It's another vicious depression cycle. A child may withdraw and isolate herself from friends and classmates, leading to loneliness, which may perpetuate the depression. Having friends and a social support system can be of great help to a child dealing with depression.

  Some schools offer after-school activities that teach a mix of social and academic skills, through activities such as noncompetitive sports, special interest clubs, or skills enhancement programs. You should encourage your child to attend one of these activities, if such a program is available.

Creating a School Team to Help Your Child

Nearly every school has personnel experienced in dealing with mental health issues. School psychologists, nurses, guidance counselors, and school social workers can be wonderful resources. Because their mandate is to assist children with school-related problems, your child may not be eligible to receive direct services if her depression doesn't directly impact her educational performance. But you can still make contact to get advice and guidance on how to handle a situation that presents difficulty for you and your child, and you can encourage an atmosphere in which everyone shares information and resources, thereby fostering a team spirit to help your child.

Some schools may even provide counseling support for your child, and this may be a reasonable option for some families. My major concern with school counseling is that too often the whole family isn't involved—the child is treated in isolation from her family. In my experience, the most effective counseling takes place when all members of the family are involved in the process. Counseling in school may be more effective for adolescents than for preadolescents because of their more advanced verbal and cognitive skills. However, even with adolescents, an attempt should be made to get the family involved in the process.

The School Psychologist

School psychology is a discipline that attempts to bridge educational psychology with clinical psychology. Psychology is a very broad field, and it is almost impossible for a school psychologist to be an expert in all areas of educational and clinical psychology. Educational psychology investigates how people learn, while clinical psychology focuses on the issues related to mental and behavioral disorders. The school psychologist typically has a master's degree or a doctorate.

From an educational perspective, a school psychologist evaluates students' academic progress and serves as an educational consultant to classroom teachers and parents. School psychologists have an understanding of how children learn and the challenges they face at various age levels. This knowledge gives them insight into appropriate and inappropriate educational practices.

From the clinical psychology perspective, a school psychologist may conduct an assessment of a child's social and emotional functioning by using structured interviews, self-concept scales, behavior rating scales, and depression rating scales. She may also use projective tests, such as family or figure drawings, to gain more insight into a child's difficulties.

The school psychologist also has the ability to observe how an individual child performs in the classroom, something a teacher would likely find difficult because she has twenty to thirty other children who require her attention. By observing a child's level of classroom participation, ability to complete classwork, compliance with teacher requests, and quality of peer interactions, the psychologist may gather information helpful in addressing the child's particular needs. The principles of behavioral assessment, which chart a child's behaviors in terms of their frequency and intensity, allow a school psychologist to prepare an objective report on how your child functions in the classroom. This data might be useful to a pediatrician or psychiatrist who is prescribing medication for your child.

School psychologists are trained to do individual and group counseling when necessary, although they don't usually conduct psychotherapy with children. Because the caseload of the typical school psychologist is so high, it's difficult for her to meet with every parent or child who needs her services. In most schools, parental concerns have to relate to a child's educational progress in order to justify the involvement of the school psychologist.

Before consulting with your school psychologist, you should clearly formulate in your own mind a description of the problem and the type of assistance you're looking for. Talking to your child and his teachers in advance will provide the details you'll need to clearly express your concerns. (I'll talk more a little later about classroom teachers and how to make them your allies in your quest to help your child.)

When you've come up with a clear statement of the problem and an idea of what kind of help you're seeking, contact the school psychologist. In most schools, this is done by making a telephone call or filling out a written referral form. The school psychologist may have a daunting caseload, so it may take a while before she can fit you into what's probably an overloaded schedule. Like all busy people, the psychologist may have a hard time setting a precise date, but be sure to ask her to give you a rough idea of when she'll contact you to set up a time to get together. If contact isn't made within that time, you should remind the psychologist that you're waiting for help. Don't be afraid to be assertive—if you let a psychologist know that you consider the situation important, that you've been waiting a while for help, and that you want a clear and firm appointment, you should get results.

You can also refer your child to the school's Committee on Special Education (CSE), if you feel that the school psychologist hasn't responded adequately to your request for assistance. This committee usually has to meet within thirty to sixty school days of your referral, which means that a psychological evaluation must be done by that time. More information on CSEs follows later in this chapter.

School Social Worker

The school social worker usually has a master's degree in social work. He's trained to work with children and families in order to resolve emotional issues that might interfere with a child's academic progress. As part of his day, he might conduct individual or group counseling with children and meet with parents. A school social worker is also required to conduct social histories (a record of the child's previous health, emotional, and family history) for children who are referred to a Committee on Special Education.

Because of his experience and training, a school social worker often is a good resource for information about different parenting strategies and ways to improve a child's emotional state. He may also serve as a case manager, coordinating counseling support services in and outside the school, referring a child to outside services for which she may eligible, such as Big Brothers or Big Sisters, YMCA programs, public counseling agencies, services for alcoholics and their families, or countywide social services.

School Nurse

The school nurse is another member of the school team who may have insight into a child's emotional and academic difficulties. Certification requirements vary from state to state, ranging from two years of post-high school education to two years of post-college education, with special courses in child development and education policy. Usually, she must also be a registered nurse.

The school nurse can be a very important person in your child's life. A child who is depressed is more at risk for feeling sick. He might have frequent stress-related illnesses that manifest in very real stomachaches or headaches. His immune system might also be weaker, predisposing him to susceptibility for contracting various illnesses.

Because of her role as healer, the school nurse may have a unique position among all school personnel. Here's someone who (usually) won't be angry if the child hasn't done his homework, won't withhold privileges if he hasn't been paying attention in class, and won't raise her voice to try to coax him into joining a class activity. Because she doesn't put pressure on a child, she may become the child's major confidante in the school system. And to seal the deal, she's always around. As a parent, you should recognize the value of including the school nurse on your team.

Guidance or School Counselor

While some elementary schools are lucky enough to have the services of a guidance or school counselor, the vast majority of guidance counselors work at the secondary level. These professionals can provide assistance regarding a child's educational program and emotional functioning. Guidance counselors typically have a master's degree in counseling psychology, which gives them a foundation for understanding a child's problems and helping to oversee their resolution. Unlike school psychologists, the guidance or school counselor's focus is on counseling and not assessment.

Because secondary students have many teachers, getting feedback on a child's progress and planning a coordinated program may be difficult. With one person—the guidance counselor, usually—coordinating the efforts of your child's teachers, chances of success go way up.

Guidance counselors are often the first line of intervention at the secondary school level. They usually consult with the school psychologist or school social worker when situations involve more exceptional types of difficulties. They are the key figures involved in monitoring and coordinating educational services in the middle and high schools. It would be difficult to plan any effective in-school intervention without their assistance.

Classroom Teacher

For most children, the adult "face" of school is her classroom teacher. Teachers, who are in everyday contact with a child, play a special role in your child's life and can make a tremendous difference in helping her feel better and alleviate the symptoms of her depression.

Teachers usually complete a four-year college program followed by a one-year master's degree program. Teachers' graduate training programs tend to focus on educational issues or on subject matter, as opposed to mental health issues. Therefore, a teacher may have little training in or understanding of mental health issues, such as depression.

A teacher's job description includes placing reasonable demands on a child to pay attention and complete her schoolwork. When a child is depressed, her focus and motivation to complete schoolwork often decreases—and not all teachers will react in the same way. The most progressive approach would be for a teacher to talk to the child alone and try to offer assistance, but some teachers may resort to punishment in the form of detention or make negative comments about a child's decline in academic performance. And as we've seen in other circumstances, punishment usually leads to a cycle of worse performance and increased negative consequences.

Again, the key is to share information about your child's depression with her teachers. In this situation, you may be in a position to educate the educators. A depressed child often has a strong need for his teachers' support. Unfortunately, his misbehavior and irritability can backfire, causing teachers to be angry and to engage in a battle of wills. While a teacher's understanding of your child's difficulties may not guarantee more sympathetic treatment for him, it will certainly increase the chances of this happening. You may be able to help the teacher see him as someone who is hurting and needs understanding instead of as being lazy or antisocial.

Teachers are also well situated to give helpful feedback regarding your child's progress and adjustment. English and art teachers may be in a position to know a lot about how your child feels. A depressed child usually doesn't draw cheery pictures with sunshine and flowers. Instead, she'll use dark colors and portray clouds and gloom, and the images will reflect her sadness. In her writing, too, she may reveal an unhealthy fascination with death or morbid details about illness or may present a pessimistic view of life.

Elementary and secondary teachers interact with a child in different ways, and parents should keep that in mind when trying to coordinate conferences and meetings. I often find it easier to coordinate with an elementary school teacher, where only one teacher is likely to be involved. In middle and high school, because each child usually has many teachers and because some teachers may look upon themselves as teachers of a subject rather than as teachers of your child, scheduling may be more difficult.

Getting Feedback on Your Child's School Performance. The Daily School Performance Questionnaire on page 145 is one way of getting regular feedback on your child's school performance from their teacher. This form takes about thirty seconds to complete, so even the busiest of teachers should be able to find the time to fill it out. The result should be that the teacher becomes more aware of your child's needs and your child has a tangible way to measure his progress, even if his depression causes him to remember only the negatives.

The questionnaire is a useful tool that not only monitors and evaluates your child's performance but can become a motivator. If your child has a "bad day," you can suggest that he let it go and then encourage him to have a "good day" tomorrow. If your child only has one good day during the week, then he can set a goal to have two good days the following week.

I've created a sample questionnaire and filled in some objectives to give you an idea of how this might work, but I recommend that you, your child, and her teachers create your own questionnaire with realistic and specific objectives that she has a good chance of achieving. For example, if your child is only completing 20 percent of her schoolwork, your objective for the first week might be for her to complete 50 percent. During the next few weeks, you should attempt to gradually increase the rate of work that she needs to complete. The danger of setting the initial performance criteria too high is that your child won't be able to make a dramatic change, will suffer yet another failure, and won't be helped to overcome her depression. Impossible demands won't help improve your child's performance.

Support Services at Your Child's School

All schools are likely to have some support services available, but the structures and the labels may be different. In the school setting, parents have many potential allies in creating a helpful, practical, positive plan for improving the situation of a depressed child.

Child Study or Teacher Team Meetings

An alternative to meeting alone with the classroom teacher or school principal is a meeting in which several educators participate. Some schools have committees, or child study teams, that meet regularly to discuss children who are experiencing difficulties in school. At these meetings, several members of the school staff—classroom teacher, school psychologist, school social worker, guidance counselor, school principal—might be present.

Even if your school doesn't do this, you might lead the way and ask the principal or guidance counselor to set up a meeting with educational support staff in order to discuss your concerns. You can pitch the idea as a troubleshooting session in which a variety of educators get together with you to brainstorm how best to help your child. Your goal might be to gather information about alternative educational options, discuss your child's social interactions, or offer whatever information you wish to share about your child's depression and her treatment.

Crisis Teams

Many school districts have crisis intervention teams (consisting of guidance counselors, school social workers, school psychologists, and the school nurse) to deal with a student who talks about suicide.

Daily School Performance Questionnaire

Child's Name _____

Week of _____

Teacher Filling Out Questionnaire _____

If the child exhibits satisfactory performance in an area, then mark it with a check. If the child does not exhibit satisfactory performance, then leave that area blank.

OBJECTIVES	MON.	TUES.	WED.	THUR.	FRI.
Classwork completed 50 percent of the time					
Refrains from fighting					
Homework completed					
Tries to answer one question in class					

Teacher Comments: _____
_____
_____
_____

Parent Comments: _____
_____
_____
_____

When a child has written a suicide note or has spoken to someone about hurting himself, one of the crisis team members talks to the child and assesses him for suicide risk. The parents will be contacted regarding the perceived risk, and the child might be referred to a hospital or a public agency with a crisis intervention unit to be assessed for further risk and possible hospitalization.

A crisis team usually meets at short notice because it wants to have a recommendation in place before the end of the school day. Very often, the team makes a determination of a child's suicide risk without initially talking to the parents, but the child's risk of hurting himself will be shared with parents and all the details of the incident will be reported. If a child is considered to be at risk of harming himself, a parent should make a real effort to follow the team's suggestions. If you feel that the team's assessment and recommendations are wrong, you should immediately make an appointment with a mental health professional you trust in order to get an independent opinion. This is not a situation in which you want to make a mistake, since your child's life could be at stake.

Section 504 Plan

Section 504 is part of federal legislation stating that any child with a documented disability must be provided with appropriate modifications and compensations in her school environment. With a depressed child, for example, the modifications might include extended testing times, a separate testing location, reading test instructions aloud to her and making sure she understands them, weekly feedback reports to parents, or counseling in the school. In order for a child to qualify for such modifications, parents must provide a statement in writing from a physician or psychologist saying that their child has been diagnosed with depression. After the documentation is provided, a meeting will be held at the school with the school psychologist and other support staff to develop a Section 504 plan and recommend appropriate modifications.

Tutoring Services

If your child's depression causes her to miss a lot of school, you can request that she be provided with a tutor to come to your home—

and the school district must pay for it. If your child broke her leg or had a physical illness that prevented her from attending school for an extended period, the school district would have to pay for a home tutor. Depression is just as much an illness as an overtly physical one, and it can just as easily prevent a child from attending school.

A tutor can be a terrific resource to keep your child from worrying about the work he's missing and avoid the stress of having to fill in gaps in learning when he eventually returns to school.

After-School Programs

Not all schools have an after-school program, but if yours does, it can be a good place for your child to socialize with other children or get extra help completing homework. Check with your child's school principal to see whether programs are available to assist with homework. If none exist, you can ask if any teachers might stay after school to help students. You might also investigate clubs or sports activities in which your child can participate, even if they aren't school affiliated. Schools are often aware of registration information for baseball, softball, soccer, football, or basketball leagues.

Committee on Special Education

When other strategies have been unsuccessful or if your child is in danger of failing in school, you might consider a referral to a Committee on Special Education (CSE). The goal of the referral is to provide your child with support services that will help him be successful in school—but there's a price. In direct contradiction to my preference for dealing with individuals and not labels, the price is that your child will be labeled and may carry that label and be judged by it for a long time.

In order to obtain special educational services, a child must be referred to a CSE, which will decide whether the child has a "handicapping condition" that interferes with his "ability to learn." Some form of this committee exists in all school systems nationwide and comprises a school psychologist, a school administrator, a teacher (typically a special education teacher), a parent of a special education student, and/or a school nurse.

The source of the referral might be a parent, a teacher, a physician, a nurse, or another related educational specialist. Once a referral is made, the CSE usually has thirty to sixty school days to set up a meeting to determine if a child qualifies for a special educational service. During this time, the psychologist must complete a psycho-educational evaluation. Information concerning events experienced by your child and the family background may be requested by the school social worker, and the results of a current physical examination will be required. If your child hasn't seen his pediatrician recently, the school might arrange for a district physician to conduct a brief examination.

Among the handicapping conditions that qualify for special education services are these categories: learning disabled, emotionally disturbed, speech impaired, mentally retarded, hard of hearing, visually impaired, orthopedically impaired, other health impaired, or multiply handicapped. Keep in mind that the label can be removed if your child makes sufficient academic progress in future school years and is moved back into the general school population.

The CSE has only two labels that can be used to classify a child with depression: other health impaired and emotionally disturbed. To my way of thinking, the label of other health impaired is not only preferable to emotionally disturbed, it's more accurate. *Emotionally disturbed* implies to teachers and administrators that your child has serious behavior control issues when, in fact, he is depressed and internalizes instead of externalizing his problems. They might think that your child is schizophrenic or more seriously impaired than he is, and this might lead them to overestimate the degree of your child's difficulties. *Other health impaired,* however, more accurately describes the situation in which a physiological condition—in this case, the body's inability to properly utilize neurotransmitters that regulate emotions and behavior—affects a child's health.

You have many rights as a parent in this process—and your child has rights, too. The school psychologist shouldn't meet with a child without parental permission. The CSE almost never labels a child without parental permission. If the CSE wants to label a child without parental permission, it would have to take the parent to an independent hearing, which would cost the school district a lot of money in legal expenses. School districts will probably only go this route in circumstances where the child presents such significant behavioral and emotional difficulties that the child's safety or that of others is at risk.

If the CSE decides that your child has a handicapping condition, she will be recommended for various support services that range from full-time placement in a small class to periodic out-of-classroom support services. The CSE, by law, has to follow the principle of a least restrictive environment. Therefore, a child who can function in a regular classroom shouldn't be placed in a small self-contained classroom with other special education students. In addition, a child with a mild difficulty shouldn't receive extensive out-of-classroom support services. Your child may also be recommended for the development of a behavior plan, school counseling, extra academic support, or the services of a teacher's aide. When you review a plan that has been developed for your child, keep in mind that the goal should be to have her placed in the most normal environment in which she can succeed.

Once the depression is successfully treated, you should arrange another CSE meeting to transition your child into an academic program that doesn't include special education support services.

Confidentiality

If you are reluctant to see a therapist because you feel that family business belongs in the family, you'll probably be even less comfortable sharing personal information with staff members at your child's school since you may not have control over who gets hold of it. Teachers may talk in the faculty room, and a staff member may hear information that wasn't meant to be shared.

First of all, keep in mind that you don't need to share personal details of your home life with school personnel. Sure, you'll want to talk about any clinical diagnosis so that your child's teachers will have a better understanding of him and be more sensitive to his emotional and academic needs—but it doesn't have to go any farther than that.

It's true that nobody can guarantee confidentiality, but I've found in my years of working both in and out of public schools that most teachers are sensitive and cooperative when a parent makes it clear that he wants to have information kept confidential.

A Plan for Parents

- ▶ Set a meeting with your child's teacher(s) or guidance counselor to discuss your concerns about your child's symptoms of depression.
- ▶ Hire a tutor if you feel your child is struggling in school.
- ▶ Don't put too much academic pressure on your child if she is very stressed out.
- ▶ Create a mechanism for getting daily or weekly feedback to monitor your child's progress.
- ▶ Call one of your child's teachers if you suspect that things aren't going well in school.
- ▶ Join your child's school Parent-Teacher Organization. The more visible and involved you are at her school, the more aware you will be of any potential difficulties.
- ▶ Look for assistance from school staff at the beginning of the school year if your child is having difficulty in school. Early intervention is the best way to ensure you will get the help you need for your child.

9

The Family as Partner

FAMILIES ARE IMPORTANT. No one will dispute that. The family is the place where the foundations of beliefs and behavior, assumptions and needs, pleasure and connectedness are built. And my primary reason for writing this book is to help families who are struggling to deal with the demands and (ultimately, I hope) the satisfactions of helping a child rise from depression.

Even the strongest family is likely to experience needless suffering and conflict unless the parents, the main navigators of the family ship, are aware of depression, what it looks like, how it affects all members of the family, and what can be done to turn things around. Childhood depression doesn't just affect the child alone. It has a tremendous impact on his parents and siblings, who may be unaware that they've been living with a clinically depressed child for several months.

To make things more complicated, when a child breaks a leg, parents usually have confidence in what they should do. Take a child to the emergency room, get x-rays, have an orthopedic doctor put the leg in a cast, and teach the child how to maneuver on crutches—it's a fairly commonplace process, and parents know more or less what to expect. They have a sense of how long the leg will take to heal and what needs to be done to make sure it heals properly.

Unfortunately, no such specific information is commonly available to parents about the course and treatment of depression. The symptoms might last a few weeks, several months, or perhaps years.

Even the psychologists and psychiatrists who first treat a child's depression can't say precisely how long the depression will take to lift or even what treatment will be the most effective for a particular child. As a result, parents feel uncertainty and doubt regarding their child's healing process.

In my mind, part of the job of the treating mental health professional is to keep a parent optimistic regarding the child's recovery. With proper treatment, nearly every child will get better. Once parents truly embrace that optimism, they're often more patient with their child, knowing that eventually things will improve and they all won't have to suffer forever. If parents hold on to a negative attitude, they're sure to communicate that to their child—which will just as surely help to perpetuate the depression.

Shifting Negative Family Responses to Positive Reactions

Some of the responses that parents and siblings might have to living with a depressed child can be shifted from positive to negative, if you can identify the reactions.

How you perceive your child will have a big impact on how you behave and how you relate to him. If you see your child as angry and defiant, you're more likely to react with anger and defiance yourself, leading to an unnecessary power struggle. But if you learn to look beyond the anger, you'll see a wounded child who is hurting and extremely sensitive. I encourage you to find a way to emotionally connect with your child so that the two of you can have a positive instead of a confrontational relationship. Look for the good aspects of your child and focus on them. Your child will work harder with you to achieve the goals you've set up if she feels that you accept, like, and care about her. But your feeling of acceptance cannot be faked. If it isn't genuine, your child will certainly know it.

Blame Game

Blame is a fruitless exercise. I still remember being at a case study meeting in which a child was the focus when the head of the clinic asked the group, "Who is to blame for this child's problems?" As soon as I heard those words, I knew any chance of the meeting being productive was gone.

Often, a depressed child doesn't have any idea why she feels so awful and may seek to blame her parents or siblings for her feelings. It's difficult for an adult to accept responsibility for feelings she neither wants nor understands, and it's even harder for a child to grasp what's going on. It's essential for parents to understand that depression is a complex interaction of genes and environment, not the result of a specific event, such as not letting your daughter go to the school dance last Friday.

I've seen more than one child try to hold his parents hostage emotionally by telling them that they're making the depression worse by not giving him what he wants. Parents who buy into this manipulation may spend a lot of money to give the child the newest video game system, for example, only to discover that the child is still depressed. If depression could be bought off, I wouldn't be seeing so many children from families that are financially comfortable. If buying your child new toys would fix depression, you'd be better off going to Toys "R" Us than to a psychologist. I've seen enough of this kind of thing to know that giving in to your child and buying toys or electronic goods (especially if you can't afford them) won't cure your child's depression. What's more likely is that things will get worse.

Don't accept blame for your child's depression. Even your child knows deep inside that you didn't cause it. It's just that when a child feels down, she's constantly looking for ways to feel better. While getting material items or special privileges may make the child feel better in the short run, those rewards won't affect long-term functioning. Depression is best treated by a mental health professional who works with the family to improve the child's situation.

Guilt

The other side of blame is guilt, a version of self-blame in which some parents might feel that their child's depression is the result of something they did or didn't do. "If only I'd been kinder/stricter/more active in PTO/less concerned about how neat his room is," the inner voice may repeat. Parents feel so responsible for their child's happiness that they believe if they'd only done something different, their child wouldn't be depressed.

Tricia carried her guilt about her child's depression until she sat in my office one day to discuss her son's progress. I'd seen fourteen-year-old James for four sessions, and each week he appeared to be moderately sad and unhappy. Tricia had revealed a history of depression on her side of the family, told me that James had felt sad and unhappy for about a year, and reported that the only stressors she could think of were the lack of communication with his father and the absence of his older brother, who had gone off to college that fall.

In counseling, I worked with James on improving communication with his father, and James felt that things were much better and he was talking more with his dad. James also came to a new level of understanding about his brother's absence, but there was still no change in his mood. He still felt unhappy and put little effort into his schoolwork.

After a while, it seemed that we'd worked on the issues that were troubling James, and he was still depressed. I told his parents that I felt his depression was the result of a genetic predisposition rather than an environmental stress. I suggested that I call his pediatrician to discuss the possibility of his taking a small dose of an antidepressant medication. While Tricia was a bit uncomfortable with the idea of trying medication, she immediately expressed relief when I told her that her son's depression appeared to be a physiological problem. Her face almost relaxed when she said, "You mean, it's not my fault?"

I had never thought that Tricia was in any way responsible for James's depression. She was a caring and competent mother who was trying her best in a difficult situation. In fact, she was doing a good job with James, and they had an excellent relationship. When she finally accepted that his depression wasn't her fault, she began to cry from the overwhelming sense of relief she felt. She was so thankful that she could drop the burden of guilt and move forward.

James was placed on 10 mg of Lexapro, and two weeks later his mood had significantly improved. After a month on the medication, he was back to normal, with no evidence of depression.

Walking on Eggshells

The parent-child relationship is usually not one based on equality. Often, the parent places demands on a child to do chores, complete homework, and follow rules for watching television or going to bed. But when a parent places demands on a child who is depressed and irritable, the parent may become the target for yelling, noncompliance, or a temper tantrum. Because a depressed child can be irritable and explosive, parents often tiptoe around the child to avoid having to deal with the emotional fallout if something they do leads to an outburst. They bottle up their feelings and can become depressed themselves. Parents in this situation are in a double bind: if they respond to their child with emotional intensity, they'll make the situation worse and become the object of a major meltdown by their child, and if they continue to tiptoe around their child, they'll feel as if they have lost control and are at the mercy of their child.

After years of watching parents try to walk this fine line, the best results I've seen come from parents who respond to their child and his irritability in a low-key way. Instead of matching your child's emotional intensity, try to be calm and businesslike and even be willing to compromise. Often, the best solution is to engage in a joint problem-solving process in which parents and child work together to come up with a solution that everyone can live with.

Mother Stress

Parents with a depressed child need to work together to provide a home environment that's conducive to fighting depression. In most families, mothers are still the primary caregiver and spend more time than fathers do interacting with a depressed child. It's not easy for a parent (or anyone else) to spend significant time with a depressed and irritable child. Negative feelings can be contagious, and the child's mother may feel ineffective and suffer from low self-esteem because she couldn't make the depression go away. She may also experience more conflict with her child because he is prickly, has a tantrum when he doesn't get what he wants, or is unable to deal effectively with negative feedback.

A father can help by being extra supportive of the child's mother. A quiet dinner for two or a pledge to stay home with the kids so Mom can take off on her own for a couple of hours can offer a real respite from the daily stress of caring for a depressed child. A husband can listen to his wife without getting defensive. The act of truly listening without giving criticism may provide a huge relief for a mother who already gets enough negative feedback from her depressed child.

Sibling Trauma

A depressed child can't be sent off to live in a cave until she's feeling better—even if her siblings wished for that. Being the sibling of a depressed child isn't easy. For one thing, with the depressed child getting so much parental attention, a sibling might feel neglected, angry, resentful, or just plain scared. A younger brother might resent a depressed sister because she's getting more than her fair share of attention in the family.

Sometimes a sibling may feel angry and resentful because his depressed sister gets special treatment, has more privileges, or isn't punished for things that would have gotten him grounded. He doesn't understand that parents have to give each child what they need at a particular time and can't give everyone equal treatment all the time. A child whose depressed sibling hits or verbally abuses him may also feel afraid. The sibling experiencing symptoms of depression feels things more intensely and may have a shorter fuse and a more intense explosion.

In some cases, a child might be afraid that his sibling will do something to harm herself. Put yourself in the mind of an eight-year-old who overhears his sister making threats to hurt herself—how scary to think that she'll actually carry out those threats. As if that weren't enough, a child might also be fearful of his sibling being hospitalized. Even when siblings fight a lot, they still worry and care about each other.

▶ Sam was twelve when I started seeing him in counseling sessions; his sister Jody was eight and his sister Julia was ten. When Sam was upset, he often hit his sisters and yelled at them. While Jody and Julia truly loved Sam, they didn't like to be around him. Unfortunately, the family lived in a small three-bedroom apartment and the girls couldn't avoid their brother. Sam acted out so frequently and with such intensity that, eventually, his sisters were afraid to be alone with him. When they wanted to watch television, Sam had control of the remote, and any attempt to change the channel or take the remote was met with physical violence. If Jody had candy, Sam would steal it from her. If Julia received presents, he pouted and became angry. Whenever he spoke to them, he teased or insulted them and called them names. His sisters were having a really hard time maintaining their positive feelings toward Sam.

When I saw the family for counseling, I asked his parents to involve Jody and Julia in the process after a couple of sessions, so that they might gain a better understanding of Sam's depression, not only for Sam's sake but also for their own. Sam, who saw his sisters as enemies who got in the way of his getting things he wanted, was so miserable that he couldn't see any of the positives that his sisters might have provided to him. But they were suffering, too. They would have loved to play games with him and spend time doing fun things together. It would have been nice to have peace and quiet at home and not have to listen to him yell all the time. Jody and Julia needed help in understanding that Sam didn't choose to be this way and that his behavior reflected the deep unhappiness he was experiencing.

As a result of the counseling, his sisters had a better understanding of what was going on, even though the abuse didn't disappear and they still found it difficult to deal with the situation. The counseling process did allow them to know that their parents were sympathetic and understanding of how they were feeling, and it gave them hope that things could improve.

After six weeks, Sam began to demonstrate significant improvement. He responded well to our counseling sessions and made good use of the strategies we discussed. He became less irritable, and his sisters reported having more positive interactions with him. He didn't become a model brother, but he was no longer abusive to them. There were still conflicts, but Jody and Julia were no longer worried about being alone with Sam.

Resolving Sibling Conflict

A parent's first priority when dealing with siblings who engage in frequent fights is to make sure that his children are safe and don't hurt one another. If a child is at risk of being hurt, a parent should separate the children and explain why that was necessary. Whenever possible, parents should avoid taking sides in a sibling conflict—the end result will be that one child is angry with you and the other thinks she got away with something and can continue to behave destructively without suffering any consequences. A parent's best strategy is to tell the children that they have to work out the conflict by themselves. If they're unable to do that, your strategy should be to remove them from the source object that stimulated the conflict. This may give them more incentive to work out the conflict without your intervention. If you have to intervene, your children will have a harder time learning the skills needed to resolve conflicts among themselves.

For example, if the conflict is over television or computer time, you can tell them that nobody will have access to the computer or television until they can work out a solution they can all abide by. Another way of dealing with sibling conflict is to engage in preventive strategies, in which rules for resource usage (televisions, computers, video games, toys) are set up in advance. The family might come up with a rule which limits a child's time on the computer to half an hour if someone else is waiting to use it. Setting things up in advance with clear rules is a good way to decrease the amount of conflict in a family.

Things can get very difficult for parents if more than one child is depressed. Mothers of siblings in this situation often suffer from feelings of depression.

▶ The first member of one family I saw was Mary, a fourteen-year-old whose initial counseling session revealed that she constantly had thoughts about hurting herself. Mary was suffering from a major depressive episode and seemed very close to needing hospitalization, but she clearly indicated that she had no plan to kill herself. Her older brother Carl had been hospitalized for depression when he was fifteen and was still seeing a therapist.

Even though Carl was no longer hospitalized, his symptoms of depression were severe, and he also experienced many mood swings. Mary never knew what to expect from him. Sometimes Carl could be the greatest brother in the world, and at other times he'd be her worst enemy, deliberately saying things that he knew would make her feel terrible.

My feeling was that Carl resented Mary because she'd been diagnosed with depression, which might lead to his losing the attention he'd been receiving from his parents. Previously, they'd spent most of their time worrying about him and trying to avoid upsetting him. Now their attention was being turned to Mary. When Mary needed him the most, Carl began to lash out at her with cruel, angry comments. He even accused her of faking depression to get sympathy from their parents. Every time Mary seemed to feel better, Carl started an argument.

One of my major concerns was to help Mary find ways to avoid letting Carl hurt her feelings. I also tried to give her insight into his behavior and help her realize that it was a function of Carl's own difficulties and not the result of anything that she was or was not doing. Having a sibling with depression made the treatment more complicated for Mary. We had to deal with her depression plus Carl's negative reaction to it.

Of course, this was an extremely difficult situation for their parents. It was hard enough when it was just Carl who was depressed, but it was significantly worse when Mary became depressed. By the time the parents came in for a session with me, they had lost almost all hope and felt beaten down. I had to work nearly as hard to help the parents deal with this situation as I did to help Mary.

During the counseling process, the parents began to regain their hope, and they worked with me to develop strategies to assist their children in feeling better and having less conflict with each other. They no longer felt that there was no point in trying. I helped them understand that things wouldn't get better in a day and that they should expect a process in which they'd see changes happening over time.

After a month, Mary no longer thought about hurting herself and reported that she felt a little better. However, she still had difficulty getting her schoolwork completed and had many conflicts with her parents. It was a slow process, taking weeks to see progress on the goals we had set. Eventually, the conflict resolution strategies we worked on were successful, and Mary's school performance was back to her old level of achievement. Mary is no longer depressed and she has a positive relationship with her parents.

Unfortunately, Carl continued to have his ups and downs. His depression was more serious and intense. However, as Mary began to get better, he also began to treat her better. It would have been nice if he could have treated her better when she was feeling depressed, but his depression prevented him from doing that.

Communication Issues

Often, the children who most need to talk to others are the ones who don't talk at all. Depressed children may avoid talking to their parents and their siblings. They're so burdened by negative feelings that they're afraid of how family members will respond if they truly share how they feel. They may also feel so irritable that other people may avoid attempting to communicate with them. I'll discuss how to improve communication in more detail in later chapters.

Depressed Parents Dealing with Depressed Children

If you have a depressed child, there is also a possibility that you yourself may have symptoms of depression. As I noted earlier, about 25 percent of the time, a depressed child has a parent who is also suffering from depression. One of the best things you can do if you have symptoms of depression is to seek treatment for yourself. It's hard for any parent to cope with a depressed child, but it's significantly harder if you are also depressed.

Depressed people tend to be sensitive and at the same time irritable. When a conflict occurs, it might engender emotions out of proportion to the problem. Reacting with strong emotion to an emotionally upset child can add fuel to an already blazing fire, making an existing condition worse. However, it may be difficult for a depressed parent to adequately control his reactions when a child is emotionally intense and on the attack. When a parent gets help for his depression, he can then respond more appropriately to his child.

A parent who is depressed should try to be open with her child and discuss depression and what it is. However, I strongly recommend that parents *do not* share feelings of suicidal ideation or discuss the personal issues of the intense stresses they're experiencing. This is more information than a child needs to know, more than he can handle. However, letting your child know that your depression often results in you feeling sad or having difficulty doing things is beneficial, because it helps the child understand and may short-circuit any guilt the child feels about being the cause of your sadness. Children, especially young ones, may feel that they're responsible for problems at home. Letting your child know that your feeling of sadness isn't his fault but is the result of an illness can be helpful. With very young children, I often refer to depression as a boo-boo that you can't see but one that hurts just as much as or even more than a boo-boo you can see. Consider Joshua's story.

▶ At fifteen, Joshua was failing all his classes in school. His mother, Rita, a pleasant woman who worked as a teacher's aide, began to cry whenever she came to my office because she felt the situation with Joshua was hopeless. Her own sense of the future was impaired, as was her son's. Rita had difficulty seeing how things could ever get better and tended to reinforce Joshua's own negative view of the future. In counseling sessions, what seemed to make a difference for Rita was the sense of hope that I was able to instill. I gave her reassurances that her son would be able to turn things around. I also worked on focusing on his positive traits at every session. Rita's habit was to focus on his negative traits and lose sight of the fact that she had a good son who was experiencing problems. Like other depressed parents, Rita had a difficult time seeing anything positive.

Joshua was generally a nice and polite boy. He didn't take drugs or engage in inappropriate behavior outside of home. With his family, he became easily angered and yelled at his parents and his sister. He rarely complied with requests from Rita because he no longer respected her ability to follow through if her requests weren't fulfilled. He did, however, respond to requests from his father because he was afraid of him. Rita felt ineffective, and the situation had begun to cause conflict in her marriage because she felt that her husband wasn't backing her up.

During my sessions with them, I tried to help the parents establish better coordination. Rita learned to choose her battles so that she could establish compliance on the issues most important to her. I worked with both parents on their communication skills. I also suggested that Rita get counseling for her own depression. She was initially resistant because she wanted to put all her focus and energy on her son. However, I told her that the best thing she could do for Joshua was to get individual counseling for herself. If her depression was successfully treated, she would have the resources to be more effective in dealing with her son. She eventually went for counseling, and her mood and attitude improved. Joshua began to treat her with more respect, and her relationship with her husband improved. It took almost a year for Joshua to get out of his depression. He passed tenth grade with a D average, and I considered that to be a good result since he'd been failing all his classes before starting counseling.

During the next school year, Joshua showed terrific improvement, achieving As and Bs in his classes. The depression had lifted for both Joshua and Rita, and their relationship became a good one.

Talking About Depression with Family and Friends

Depression is a concept that's still not widely understood. Family members or friends may contradict a doctor's diagnosis and say that a child is simply lazy or stubborn. I worked with one child whose divorced parents disagreed with each other over my diagnosis of depression. While the mother felt comfortable with the diagnosis, the father felt threatened by it. He felt that the diagnosis of depression implied that his son was weak and that it somehow reflected upon him. He refused to consider treatment options such as counseling or medication because he didn't agree that his son's situation warranted treatment. Instead, the father made his own diagnosis—his son was lazy. The treatment was that he just needed someone (that is, his mother) to get on his case to motivate him.

Sometimes it's easier to blame someone else or come up with an alternative explanation for a child's problems than it is to accept that a child has an emotional illness that needs treatment. I continued to see the father and educated him on what depression was. Eventually, he came to understand what I was trying to do and supported my treatment plan. His son got better—and several months later, the father sent me a letter thanking me for my help.

Many children are sensitive about sharing information about their personal lives outside of their family. They may not want their aunts, uncles, or grandparents to be aware of what they're feeling. When a parent shares information about a child's depression, it's important to be sensitive to the child's feelings and to be aware of the person to whom the information is going.

For teens, it's helpful for parents and child to discuss the issue of what information can be shared and with whom. And whether you're discussing the problems of a young child or a teen with a relative or a friend, it's important that you make it clear that this is confidential information and shouldn't be shared with other acquaintances.

A Plan for Parents

▸ Have a family discussion about what depression is and isn't, and emphasize that a depressed person doesn't simply choose to feel that way.

▸ Go out on a date with your partner or take one evening a week to do something for yourself. You'll be more effective with your child if you are at your best and aren't stressed.

▸ Call a friend when you're feeling tense.

▸ Find one positive thing your child does each day, and bring it to his attention.

▸ Make a list of adjectives to describe your child. Afterward, look at the negative terms you used and try to change them into something kinder and more understanding.

▸ Schedule time for your family to go on outings together—to a park or a movie, for example.

▸ Give each of your children special alone time with a parent each night when you play a game or talk to them. If you don't have a lot of time, try to set aside even a few minutes for this activity.

▸ Try to take the perspective of other members of your family and imagine how they are feeling.

10

Creating a
Supportive Environment

I'VE ALREADY SAID that depression appears to be the result of the interaction between genetic predisposition and environment. While we can't change our child's DNA or prevent all stress from entering his life, we can structure an environment that discourages depression. The strength of a child's genetic predisposition for depression and the events that take place outside the home are beyond a parent's control, but other factors that parents *can* influence play important roles in childhood depression.

Parents can take an active role in using strategies that may minimize the likelihood that ordinary sadness will develop into depression, that depression will get worse, and that depression will reoccur.

The Positive Power of Good Habits

I'm a big believer in developing good habits and firm limits that all family members understand and agree with. So many conflicts at home can be avoided by having clearly accepted routines and expectations. In some ways, developing family routines is like having a blueprint before you start building a house—plans are drawn, everyone has an idea of her part in the process, chaos is avoided, and the end result is that you've built something that provides a harmonious haven for healthy growth, fun, and the nurturing of strong family bonds.

Having clear and well-established routines helps lessen stress, conflict, and anxiety in your home and promotes success and confidence. When things are predictable, you don't have to worry about when they will happen. You also don't have to argue about when and how things should be done. And the added bonus—for everyone— is that when a child sticks with the routine, his parents don't have to get on his case about doing what is expected.

When bad habits have become the routine, breaking them takes some real effort, but they can be broken and the results will be worth the work.

Your child may be initially resistant to your efforts to establish good habits. Change can be hard for a child, especially when the change isn't to her liking. And that's the key: if you don't impose new ways of doing things but instead actively involve your child to develop positive routines at home, you're likely to meet much less resistance. After all, what good are clear guidelines if your child resists them and they can't be enforced?

Your power as a parent is dependent, at least in part, on your child's willingness to accept your authority and your rules. Just as good business managers understand the concept of buy-in, parents need to know that a child who feels that she's had some input into the creation of the rules and routines is much more likely to be cooperative, if not necessarily enthusiastic.

Cultivating these good habits will help a depressed child sleep, do homework, exercise, keep busy, help others, build positive peer relationships, and communicate.

Sleep

Think back to the last time you went through a stretch of not getting enough sleep and having too much to do. Maybe you snapped at your spouse, got easily distracted at work and felt anxious about completing a project, or experienced a scary lapse while driving. You felt annoyed, jittery, unfocused, and less engaged in pursuits and people you normally find interesting.

Only the details change when it's a child who doesn't get adequate sleep. Most children require nine hours of sleep to function at their best. A tired child is apt to find dealing with everyday stress more difficult than one who's rested. He's likely to be irritable, get into conflicts with family members and peers, have problems paying attention, and have difficulty completing schoolwork. Fatigue affects a child's energy level and his motivation to deal with daily responsibilities. The resulting negative impact on his academic performance and interpersonal relations might serve as a trigger for developing or increasing the symptoms of depression.

A child who is alert and rested is better able to deal with academic demands, interpersonal conflict, and the ordinary disappointments of her daily life routine. I don't have to tell you that a well-rested child is much easier for a parent to deal with than a tired and cranky one. The well-rested child usually travels a more positive track, earning more positive feedback from others and responding better to this feedback.

When a parent establishes clear bedtime routines and sticks to them, children generally accept them with a minimum of fuss. A child who can go to sleep at a different time each night may try to stay up much later than he should. As a rough guideline, I suggest the following bedtimes:

Preschoolers to fifth graders	8:00
Sixth to eighth graders	9:00
Ninth to twelfth graders	10:00

On the weekends, the times can be extended for an hour since a child can sleep longer in the morning. These are rough guidelines, since some variability exists in the amount of sleep that individual children need.

If your child falls asleep near the designated time, that tells me she needs to go to sleep at that time. If she can't get to sleep, try moving her bedtime to half an hour later. But don't let her turn on the light and play games or watch television after her designated bedtime—the result is likely to be bad habits and poor sleeping patterns.

Helping Your Child Get to Sleep. You can try experimenting with different inducements to help your child relax at bedtime. Taking a warm bath, drinking warm milk, or reading a book half an hour before bedtime may be beneficial. Perhaps she needs some background noise to get to sleep; playing soft music on a CD player or radio may help. And avoid having your child drink caffeinated soda or eat a heavy meal too close to bedtime.

The Worry Chair. If your child still can't fall asleep easily, tell her that she's still getting some rest because her eyes are closed and she's lying down. With some children, I recommend what I call a worry chair. The child gets out of bed and sits in a rather uncomfortable chair with her eyes closed and worries. After she is done worrying and is tired, she should get back into bed and go to sleep. I want a child to associate the bed with good sleeping and the chair with worrying or having trouble falling asleep.

Bad Dreams. When a child tells me he's having bad dreams, I suggest that he start his own dream and think of something that makes him feel good, happy, and relaxed. If he's afraid of monsters, then I suggest that he dream about defeating the monsters so that they go away. Over the years, one of my most effective strategies for helping a child deal with imaginary monsters is to tell him it takes an imaginary weapon to defeat the monsters. Very often, a child dreams up a weapon that disintegrates the imaginary monsters and at the same time vaporizes his fears so he can feel safe in his own room.

Homework

Establishing a set time for homework can reduce conflict at home and help a child be consistent in completing his assignments. Usually, the best time to get homework done is right after school. Then he can relax and enjoy the rest of the day and evening. But he may want to watch a particular television show or take part in a special after-school activity. Parents can be flexible about the time, as long as the routine is clear and consistent. For example, he can do his homework after dinner, as long as he finishes it all at that time.

Even with this flexibility, though, it's not a good idea to let him leave his homework until late at night. A child is likely to be most fatigued just before going to bed, and the quality of his concentration and his work won't be high. He's also under a lot of pressure when he saves homework for the last minute. A child with a tendency for depression doesn't need that feeling of being overwhelmed and being a failure.

It's helpful for parents to have their own routine regarding their child's homework. Even if you're a working parent, you can still set aside time for your child to tell you about her school day, go over her assignments, and ask for any help she might need. In addition to being part of a good routine, this serves as a foundation for good communication.

Exercise

When you ask an adult why he goes to the gym regularly, he'll probably say that he wants to keep fit and that exercise helps him cope with the demands of his busy life. Having a physical outlet can be very helpful for a child, too. Many of the depressed adolescents I've worked with have dramatically reduced their symptoms of depression when they got involved with significant physical exercise, such as lifting weights, wrestling, football, basketball, kickboxing, karate, aerobics, swimming, or running.

One seventeen-year-old boy who came to me for counseling wasn't responding to treatment. Our sessions didn't seem to have much effect on his depression. It was only when he began to go to the gym to lift weights that his depression began to dissipate. I've also seen several adolescents who became depressed after they received an injury that prevented them from playing sports. I began to wonder whether a child became depressed because of her injury or whether the physical exercise served as a means of inoculating a child from a predisposition to be depressed. I still don't know the answer, but what I do know is that exercise is often a significant part in a child's (and an adult's!) recovery from depression.

Regular exercise not only helps a child establish good habits that will serve him well as an adult, it also helps to improve a child's mood by releasing endorphins, those hormones that help a person feel better. And if all that weren't enough, in addition to the direct positive physical effect, exercise can boost a child's self-esteem by giving him a more positive image of his abilities and his physical appearance.

Getting Started with Exercise. To help a child get started on an exercise program, it is sometimes helpful to make it a family activity. You can take brisk walks together and spend quality time talking to your child as well as improving your own physical condition.

If your child persists in being unwilling to engage in physical activities, it might be time to have her checked out by a physician to rule out any physical problems. If nothing is physically wrong, a child's resistance to exercise might be the result of her lack of energy. A significantly depressed child often avoids the suggestions that might help her feel better because she simply doesn't have the energy to invest in them. If that seems to be the case, start slowly—a short walk, even if it's accompanied by grumbles, is a beginning. You can increase the time or the distance every few days and gradually work up to an effective exercise program.

Keeping Busy

A child sitting alone in his room may be daydreaming, trying to solve a problem, pouting, or worrying, while a depressed child sitting alone in his room is likely to be caught in a cycle of negative thoughts.

On the other hand, a child busy with activities that engage him with other people and new ideas has less time to focus on negative experiences. You can help your child stay busy by enrolling him in youth or church organizations, after-school clubs, or sports activities, introducing him to a new hobby, or taking family trips to local places of interest or to visit relatives. Several children I work with have been able to manage their depression effectively by keeping busy with such activities as learning pottery, joining 4-H groups or Girl Scouts or Boy Scouts, and building model airplanes. Other children are helped by simply spending time with their friends.

There's a difference, however, between keeping busy in a positive way and simply passing time. Playing video games or spending time on the computer isn't especially effective in helping a child's mood. While it may occupy his time, these activities probably won't help him feel better—rather than interacting with other people or exploring his interests, he's zoning out. In my experience, there's no substitute for personal interactions with others when it comes to feeling better.

Helping Others

The famous psychologist Milton Erickson once described an unhappy, depressed, and isolated older woman who was able to connect with her community by growing plants and giving them away. People loved the plants and appreciated her efforts and began to respond to her positively. Their reaction caused her to respond back with warmth and openness, instead of with her usual withdrawal and gloom.

The act of giving one's time or attention to others often results in better social connections and relationships. It can also lead to increased feelings of self-esteem and self-worth. For a depressed child who has difficulty feeling good about herself, helping others can make all the difference. When a child believes that she's doing something of value, she will feel that she is a valued person.

As a parent, you might give some thought to assessing your child's strengths so you can use them to create a situation in which he can help other children or adults. Helping situations can be structured through a religious organization, school, or community center. If your child has a good command of a particular school subject, perhaps he can tutor other students. If he's good in sports, maybe he can volunteer to help coach younger children or work in a camp. If he's a good listener, you might be able to arrange for him to volunteer at a retirement home to spend time with the elderly.

Positive Peer Relationships

People are social beings and generally have a need to connect with one another. Most children are happier when they have other children to play with. Play is a central component of childhood, and children learn many things from their play activities with peers. They learn to share, compromise, and communicate with others. These are difficult skills to teach in a counseling or home environment. They're best learned through exposure in a child's natural environment. A child can't learn the give-and-take involved in social relationships by studying it or having someone describe it to him. He needs to experience social situations in his everyday life.

A child's friends and peer group can help lessen the effects of depression—or they can make it worse. Most children want friends they can talk to and play with. Having stable, supportive friends provides a child with a sense of belonging and self-worth, as well as serving as an effective outlet for expressing her feelings. But negative peer relationships may increase depression. And without friends, a child's negative opinion about herself may be reinforced.

Many parents feel upset when their child complains of having no friends. They're likely to become even more upset if their child spends time with friends they don't approve of. While you can't create friends for your child, you can create situations in which he can connect with other children, through church or youth groups or by involving extended family, such as cousins, who may be the same age. You can enroll your child in sports leagues, Boy Scouts or Girl Scouts, or dance classes. You can suggest that he invite a friend or even a relative to play.

Another possibility is to contact your child's school to see if they offer social skills counseling groups. The most effective groups are those that include high-status peers who have good social skills that can be modeled. Enrolling your child in a social skills group that only includes children with poor social skills is likely to be ineffective. She will end up feeling stigmatized and won't be exposed to real-life skills she can then adapt for her own.

Greg, a sixteen-year-old who was referred to me for counseling for depression, was making only mild progress. His friends spent a lot of time drinking and smoking marijuana and had more than a passing interest in satanic rituals. Greg didn't necessarily want to engage in these antisocial behaviors, but he had no other friends. His friends weren't at all helpful or understanding about his feelings of sadness, and his drinking and smoking seemed to make his depression worse. Only after Greg met Rick, another boy at school, who invited him to join his church youth group, did things begin to change. Greg was exposed to a group of friends who didn't drink, smoke, or engage in antisocial behavior. To his surprise, he also found comfort in going to church and having something positive to believe in. After two months, his depression lifted, and Greg felt good about himself and his new friends, who brought out the best in him.

For many children, belonging to a church, synagogue, mosque, temple, or other youth group is a means of accessing good friends and social supports. This is especially true for teenagers, who may be exploring different worlds and seeking a social group they can relate to.

Communication

One of the main reasons a child doesn't share his feelings with his parents is that he's worried about the reaction he'll get. Well-meaning but misinformed parents might tell their child that he doesn't really feel so bad and end up denying his feelings. The parents are too uncomfortable to acknowledge that their child is so unhappy. Often, a parent takes on responsibility for this unhappiness when, in fact, the child's feelings are totally independent of anything the parent has or has not done. A parent may blame herself—and then she's no longer focused on what her child is trying to communicate.

It's important to remember that if you are the average well-intentioned parent and you don't abuse your child physically or emotionally, your child's depression isn't your fault.

You should always acknowledge your child's feelings, no matter how difficult that might be. Otherwise, good communication with your child just isn't possible—and without good communication, you can't help him. There may be times when you need to let your child know that some situations are inappropriate for certain discussions. One of my patients, who wasn't suicidal, often talked about being dead in front of his five-year-old sister, who became frightened by his talk.

Sharing feelings of depression, especially really morbid thoughts or images, is best done in private and not in a public place. If your child starts to share negative feelings, gently assure him that you want to hear what he has to say, and then suggest that you go to a private place to continue the conversation.

By improving communication, children and parents have the opportunity to keep situations manageable instead of letting them balloon into overwhelming problems. When children and parents do not attempt to resolve problems as they occur but instead avoid them, the molehill will soon loom as a gigantic mountain, and climbing it will seem impossible, engendering unnecessary stress.

Creating a Special Listening Time. I encourage parents to set aside a special listening time with their child, preferably in the evening, when there are no distractions, so the child gets their full attention and has the opportunity to discuss problems without fear of punishment or ridicule. Haim Ginott, a famous psychologist, was one of the first to talk about the need for parents to give children special time to listen. Keep in mind that as a parent, you needn't have the goal to fix your child's depression yourself—the professionals your family is working with should have the experience and the knowledge to guide that process. But you do play an important role in helping your child get better by listening to her and letting her know that you understand and accept what she's feeling. During this special listening time, your child gets to talk, but you only get to listen.

Try it sometime. It's hard. At first you want to jump in and offer solutions or comfort or express anger or disappointment. And when you're doing that, you're not truly listening. If you end up criticizing or punishing your child for what she says during this time, she's likely to shut down and not share problems she finds troubling.

One child I worked with was afraid to tell her mother that she'd gotten a 52 on a math exam. Her mother wanted to know if she could ground her daughter because of her failing grade. When I asked the mother how often her daughter confided in her about poor grades or other difficulties, she was puzzled. That never happened, she informed me. I then asked her daughter whether she'd talk about school difficulties in the future if she were to be punished. She said she'd tell her mother nothing. I helped her mother understand that her daughter's sharing of information about her failing math grade was a positive sign that their communication had improved. Her daughter didn't like to get failing grades, and it was a relief to be able to discuss her problems without fear of being punished. By the end of our session, the mother understood that instead of being in punishment mode, she needed to practice being a better listener so she could work cooperatively with her daughter, instead of working against her.

Communication is such an important issue that all of Chapter 13 is devoted to offering strategies and ideas for parents.

Dealing with Trauma in Your Child's Life

If a child has suffered a significant loss or hurt, parents can help by making sure that his emotional issues are addressed. Don't postpone seeking help if you see that your child is withdrawn, irritable, or showing any of the other signs I've spoken about earlier. Go with your instincts and seek help from a mental health professional if you see your child having adjustment problems after a traumatic event. Traumatic events can come into a child's life in many different forms.

Strategies for Creating a Supportive Environment

- Have your child make a list of events that cause him to feel high stress.
- Have your child make a list of events or activities that seem to reduce her stress.
- Make a list of activities that your child likes to engage in by himself.
- Create a list of activities you and your child can do together. You might engage in one activity a day that your child looks forward to, such as baking cookies, watching a video, or playing a game.
- Create a list of situations that cause stress in your household, and have a family discussion on how they can be improved.
- Make a list of activities that your child is not currently engaged in but would like to try in the future.

The Death of a Family Member or Close Friend

Death is difficult for anyone to deal with. Sometimes parents themselves have difficulty dealing with death and want to spare their child from experiencing grief. However, just as death can't be prevented, grief also can't be avoided if you lose someone you love.

When a child loses someone important to him, parents should make sure to include him in the grieving process. Some parents feel that they're being kind to the child by shielding him and excluding him from the mourning process. But unprocessed grief, hidden in the dark and left to fester, may well grow into a serious emotional wound that may take extraordinary measures to heal years later. I encourage parents to let their children be full participants in the grieving process and have a chance to say good-bye to their loved one.

Divorce or Parents' Separation

Sometimes children feel that they're responsible for their parents' divorce or separation. They may think, "If I'd been better behaved . . . If I got better grades in school . . . If I'd done my chores . . . If

I didn't fight with my sisters and brothers . . . If I were pretty/hand-some/smart/athletic/funny . . . maybe Mom and Dad would still be together." In my practice, I've counseled numerous children who spend a lot of time trying to figure out how to get their parents back together, and it's always a challenge to help them realize that the parental split was the result of factors outside of their control. In other instances, parents have brought their children to me when they were starting the process of separation or divorce, just to make sure their children would have support available to them during a difficult time. When parents are going through a divorce, they're likely to be under great stress, so when their children need them most, it's hard for them to be there for them. Having a counselor available to meet with a child can help him to communicate his feel-ings and provide a place to work out the emotional difficulties. How much better it is to go through this short-term process than to find out later that big problems weren't effectively addressed and now have become even bigger.

Sexual or Physical Abuse

Any child who has been the victim of sexual or physical abuse should be involved in counseling. At the risk of seeming overly dramatic, I'd say that it's impossible to minimize the negative effects that such abuse is likely to have on a child. Untreated, an abused child is at high risk for suffering from deep and ongoing depression. A child who has been sex-ually abused might have feelings ranging from believing the abuse was her fault to extreme anger at the abuser. Sexual abuse is a violation of both one's body and one's soul and takes a tremendous toll on a child's self-esteem and feelings of security. This is especially true if the abuse was committed by a family member or a friend, someone the child looked up to and trusted. The result may be an inability to trust others, leaving the child with the terrible burden of keeping dark secrets and feelings inside. Sexual abuse can rob a child of her innocence and lead her to isolate herself and not connect with the normal peer and family supports. All of these reactions may be magnified when the abused child goes through puberty and is expected to begin dating other adolescents.

A Move to a New Home with a New School

Moving can be stressful for a child, especially when it involves a change in friends and schools. This is especially true for adolescents in high school. Making new friends and fitting into a new social situation can pose a real challenge for many children, particularly those with a predisposition to depression. A change in schools might also lead to academic stress, because the new teacher is covering different material than the child learned in his old school. When a family moves, it's helpful to keep lines of communication open and listen to how your child feels about the move. While the move may be unavoidable, it's better to address your child's feelings early and help ease the transition of the move.

Illness or Accident

In my practice, I see many children who become depressed as a result of a prolonged illness or an accident. The illness or physical accident may involve a significant change in the child's functioning. She may not be able to engage in activities she previously enjoyed and may have less contact with peers. Then there's the added stress that results from missing school and having to make up work assignments. The longer the problem lasts, the higher the risk for depression.

Sometimes parents focus too much on the obvious physical ailment and don't pay attention to a child's internal stress. Of course, parents need to ensure their child's physical health, but at the same time, it's important to be aware of the potential for emotional repercussions and meet those problems directly, before they become scars that may mar a child's recovery and growth.

Significant Bullying or Teasing

Being bullied or subjected to constant teasing can erode a child's self-esteem and sense of well-being. Some children who try to avoid going to school are responding to the stress of having to deal with peers who hurt their feelings every day. You shouldn't tolerate this situation if it's happening at school. Your child has the right to be educated in a safe environment and to feel secure when he goes to school. If he doesn't feel safe and secure, you should contact the school principal and insist that something be done to stop the bullying or teasing. If you don't get a satisfactory response, don't stop there—take your concerns to the school superintendent or your local school board.

Let your child know that you're in his corner—but also make sure that he's actively involved and agrees with the steps you'll be taking to remedy the school situation. Sometimes you can make the situation worse if you act out of anger and start calling other children's parents without your child's permission. The best way to handle this situation is to have your child included in the meeting with the school principal so he's aware of and comfortable with the actions that will be taken. If your child's uncomfortable, have the principal reassure him that no backlash will be tolerated. If he is still uncomfortable, don't be afraid to look for a compromise that would make him feel better.

It's important for your child to know that the school will actively work to protect him. I have found that most bullying situations can be remedied if parents and children make use of the support services available at the school.

Academic Problems at School

A child who's having learning problems in school is a good candidate for an extra load of stress, and this is especially true if he's intelligent. Think of how you'd feel if you had to go to work every day and were unable to effectively do your job. While you might look for another job, your child doesn't have that option. He has to continue to go to work in an environment in which he meets a lot of failure. If your child has learning difficulties, it's important to address them early, before they have a major impact on his self-esteem.

Early intervention is important because it prevents the development of bad habits and poor motivation. Very often, a child doesn't put forth her best effort when she lacks confidence in her ability to succeed. The less she tries, the farther she falls behind and the more she feels like a failure. The only way a child can develop a positive attitude about school is to be engaged in tasks at which she can succeed. You need to make sure your child's teachers are presenting a curriculum that your child understands and has the ability to undertake successfully.

If you suspect that your child has a learning problem, you can contact a school psychologist. Every school or school district has one, and you can call the main office at your school or the special education department in your school district to obtain his number. If the school psychologist doesn't respond to your call, you might initiate a special education referral, which would force the school district to conduct an evaluation within sixty school days. If you aren't happy with the school evaluation, you have a legal right to obtain an independent evaluation from a private psychologist at the school district's expense.

Most school psychologists will be responsive to a parent's call for help. I always appreciate a parent who seeks ways to get help for his child. I'm always more concerned and frustrated when I see a child who needs help and a parent isn't interested in working with the school.

World and Local Events

Events like war, kidnappings, and school massacres can cause a lot of anxiety and stress in children. While these events may not directly affect the life of the average child, they may have a serious impact on a child who is prone to anxiety and depression. A depressed child is more fragile and sensitive than the typical child of his age. Everything he hears or sees can have a big effect on what he thinks and feels. When a depressed child is overloaded with scary media images, the result can be bad dreams, excessive negative feelings, and increased feelings of insecurity.

If you're living with a depressed child, it's probably best to control what comes into the house via your television. Don't have the news on all night during a period of domestic or international crisis. Turn the television off or change the channel if the content is disturbing, and then turn it back on when your child isn't in the room.

But this doesn't mean that you should ignore these events in your household. Other children are bound to talk about them, so it's best to prepare your child by having a brief, simple conversation about the situation. If your child has questions, the best policy is to respond to her questions and her level of knowledge with the simplest statements that answer the questions. Don't try to introduce more information than your child has asked for. And never dismiss your child's intense reactions to media events as being silly or unimportant. Sometimes these feelings can be more intense than you can imagine, and the only way to find out about them is to seriously listen to your child and accept her feelings as being legitimate. When you listen to your child's feelings and reassure her that she is safe, you are helping her cope with her fears.

A Plan for Parents

- ► Set up a regular exercise or walk schedule for your child. Ideally, this could become a family activity.
- ► Review the times you and your child have set up for completing homework and going to sleep.
- ► Monitor your child's sleep patterns.
- ► Don't let little problems grow into big ones.
- ► Ask your child if she has experienced any traumatic events.
- ► Contact your local county recreation department to see if it has leisure or camp activities for your child.
- ► Take family vacations.
- ► Look into joining a church, synagogue, temple, or mosque that has an active youth group.
- ► Sign your child up to participate in adult-supervised activities with peers, such as Boy Scouts, Girl Scouts, or sports teams.
- ► Find out what your child's strengths are and nurture them.

11

Resolving Conflicts

THE EFFORT AND reasoning abilities required to communicate effectively and resolve conflict with a depressed child are enough to make some parents throw up their hands and say, "I give up." Depressed children are often snappish and irritable and lack the patience to listen to negative feedback from any source. In an effort to solve the problem, a parent may try explaining and negotiating and reasoning, only to find himself on a slippery slope that leads to a worsening of the conflict he was trying to avoid in the first place.

The Problem with Overexplaining

It may seem contradictory, but sometimes talking too much is as ineffective as saying too little. What is important is what you say, when you say it, how you say it—and, especially, how you listen. I've helped many parents find the road to a middle ground in which parent and child can work collaboratively to resolve conflict.

▶ Roberta, a sixteen-year-old girl, was very unhappy and couldn't handle any kind of negative feedback from her parents, David and Laura. She constantly demanded that her parents do things for her. When she was feeling down, she wanted them to take her to the mall to go shopping—right *now*. Whenever they told her she couldn't stay up late or have a new CD, her immediate response was to throw a tantrum and tell her parents that they didn't really care about her. Roberta's parents made numerous

183

trips to the mall with her and gave her CDs, sweaters, a leather backpack, and expensive jeans and sneakers, but nothing made a dent in Roberta's demands. No matter how much they gave her, it was never enough.

David and Laura were frustrated by their inability to please Roberta—she was wearing them out. Even Roberta was getting tired of the fighting. Luckily, she was able to give me insight into what was happening. It made her angry when her parents tried to explain why they couldn't give her what she wanted. The more they talked, the angrier Roberta became, and what began as a small conflict often escalated into a huge one. Roberta wanted her parents to stop trying to explain themselves and simply let her know, once and without a big fuss, that this time she wouldn't be getting what she wanted.

Roberta, David, and Laura all had to make adjustments to help ease the conflict. David and Laura had to learn how to keep their message simple and clear and say no without overexplaining. As part of the deal, Roberta had to work at disengaging from her parents when they told her no, walking away from them instead of harassing them into changing their minds.

Eventually, we all understood that Roberta wasn't intentionally trying to upset her parents. She was just constantly sad and was looking for something to fill her emotional void.

Encouraging a Depressed Child to Share Feelings

A depressed child may be afraid to tell her parents how she truly feels. It's hard to resolve a conflict with someone who doesn't let you know how she's feeling. She might be experiencing scary thoughts and may think her parents will misunderstand her and think she's crazy. She might also feel guilty about her feelings and not want to burden her parents with them. Some children are what I call cheap with their feelings. They feel that they'll have to pay a big price if they share them. They simply don't trust other people to respond appropriately to expressions of their true feelings. A child may fear that her parents will share her feelings with others, when she prefers to have them kept private. It's critical that you establish a relationship with your child that allows her the freedom to share her feelings without fear of consequences.

You can decrease defensiveness and increase open communication by accepting your child's feelings. You don't have to accept her actions, but you do have to accept her feelings. A defensive person can't listen to what another person has to say. Learn to talk about a problem in ways that don't make your child defensive. Describe the problem without blaming or labeling your child. Focus on problems that need to be fixed in a very impersonal way. If your child has made a mess in the kitchen, don't yell at her. Instead, ask her to come to the kitchen and point out, verbally and with gestures, that there's food on the floor. Describe only what you see. Try saying, "There's food spilled on the floor," and not, "You always make such a mess."

Conflicts Can Become Power Struggles

Conflicts can easily turn into power struggles in which the apparent issue isn't nearly as important to the participants as who wins. Power struggles can be avoided when parents and children have a commitment to work together and respect one another's feelings. Mary Sheedy Kurcinka, in her latest book on power struggles, *Kids, Parents, and Power Struggles*, suggests that parents provide their children with choices. When a child feels that he has some control over his life, he's more likely to cooperate.

Kurcinka also offers a new way to think about power struggles. Instead of being battlegrounds, conflicts might be peacemaking opportunities that allow you to emotionally connect with your child. The Chinese character for *crisis* combines the characters for *danger* and *opportunity*, an apt description for a parent's choices regarding power struggles.

Two Models for Conflict Resolution

One of the strategies that I've shared with parents in my private practice combines two well-respected models of conflict solving. The first model is Dr. Ross Greene's ABC Basket system. Dr. Greene, one of the top behavioral specialists in the country, wrote a book called *The Explosive Child*. The second model is Dr. Haim Ginott's Joint Problem-

Solving method. Dr. Ginott has written several books, the most widely read of which is *Between Parent and Child.*

Dr. Greene's Basket Model

In *The Explosive Child,* Dr. Ross Greene talks about putting a child's problem into one of three different baskets. By going through this mental sorting exercise, a parent decides which issues aren't negotiable, which can be dropped, and which might benefit from a collaborative solution. It's almost like dividing the things that are cluttering your closets into piles of things you need, things you can toss, and things you want to think about. In my private practice, I've found that parents who use this model experience fewer conflicts and less stress with their children.

- **Basket A.** In basket A you put issues that you can let go of, ones that don't require you to have a conflict with your child. For example, if your child doesn't want to eat his peas, let it go. Basket A is for those issues that don't involve safety or morality and don't result in distress or inconvenience to you or other family members. When you put issues in basket A, you are essentially deciding not to fight with your child over the small stuff. Not everything needs to be a battle. If you choose your battles carefully, you—and your child—won't feel as though you're in a constant state of war.
- **Basket B.** These issues usually involve convenience. Either you or your child wants something from the other, and not getting that thing is likely to lead to significant conflict. The desired item might be going to the mall, visiting a friend, getting up on time, or going to the store to get something a parent needs to make dinner. The best way to resolve basket B items is to work out a solution that you and your child can live with. The means of accomplishing this solution will be discussed in the next section, on joint problem solving. It's not magic, although it seems to be when you do it right and see it in action in your own family.
- **Basket C.** According to Dr. Greene, these issues involve safety. They're ones that you can't compromise on. In my own practice,

I also suggest to parents that they add issues of moral values to basket C. I don't think parents should compromise on their child's safety or their moral values. Basket C items might include the use of drugs or alcohol, staying out past curfew, physical aggression, school attendance, stealing, lying, or driving without permission.

When you apply this system, you'll probably discover that some situations you previously identified as problems are so unimportant that they become nonissues (basket A) and some situations are so important that they become nonnegotiable (basket C). Everything else that constitutes a source of conflict—all those everyday differences about homework, television, friends, bedtime, chores (I'll stop here because the list can get very long and we're all familiar with it!)—are left in basket B. The next strategy will offer a new way to approach those issues, one that relies on collaboration rather than "clobberation."

Dr. Ginott's Joint Problem-Solving Method

Dr. Haim Ginott, child psychologist and author of *Between Parent and Child*, endorsed joint problem solving as the preferred method for resolving conflicts between parents and children.

It's normal—and it's perfectly fine—for people living and working together to have conflicts and disagreements. What's not acceptable is for people in a disagreement to be disrespectful and insulting. People can disagree and also resolve their conflicts in many different ways.

- **Respect is required.** If you're engaged in a conflict with someone who ignores your feelings and is insulting to you, you're not likely to try very hard to resolve the conflict cooperatively. Instead, you may become confrontational, or in an attempt to avoid the confrontation, you may give in. In either case, you'll probably harbor a huge pile of resentment toward the other person. Disagreements are most likely to be resolved when people express their feelings appropriately and try to consider the needs of the other person.

- **Look for a win-win condition.** Here's one of the keys: avoid win-lose situations. Strive for a win-win condition. If you undermine your child's self-respect and sense of dignity, you're creating a situation in which a negative relationship is likely to flourish between you and your child. If, on the other hand, you can forge a solution in which everyone is heard, everyone is respected, and everyone creates a new future together, you're laying the groundwork for a strong, cohesive family culture and giving your child wonderful experience in how to approach some of life's thorniest problems.
- **Deal with one thing at a time.** One note of caution: it's important to address only one issue at a time. This isn't a time to bring up every single thing you think needs changing in your family. Start with one problem, work on it, enjoy the success, and then after some time has passed, choose the next important issue you feel needs to be addressed.

The Five Steps of Joint Problem Solving

This five-step process takes some practice, but the results are worth it!

Step 1: Identify the Problem

Each person gets a chance to explain in his own words and from his perspective what the problem is. First, one person talks, while the others listen without interrupting to comment or to press a different point of view. Then, each person has the same opportunity to express his views about the problem. At this point, nobody is offering a solution, and nobody should be defending his past behavior. It's simply a time to pay complete attention to what each person has to say about the nature of the problem. By the end of this step, the goal is to agree on a definition of the problem.

For example, Larry, who is thirteen, hasn't been finishing his homework and has been getting poor grades in school as a result. Larry tells his parents that he thinks the problem is that his parents constantly nag him to get his homework done. His parents identify the problem as Larry's inability to take responsibility for getting his homework completed. They talk about the situation until they come up with a mutually acceptable definition they can all agree on: the problem is getting the homework completed.

Step 2: List the Possible Solutions

Each parent and the child separately make a list of as many possible solutions for the problem as they can come up with. Anyone who's participated in a brainstorming session knows that sometimes what seems like a far-out idea can be a stepping-stone to a workable solution, so it's important to avoid too much self-censoring and to encourage creative thinking. Here's a place where quantity counts—everyone should try to write down as many solutions as possible.

For example, Larry might write:

- My parents will leave me alone.
- I will stay up later to do my homework.
- I will get extra money for getting my homework done.
- I'll finish just enough homework so that I can just pass.

His parents might write:

- Larry won't go out with his friends until the homework is completed.
- Larry won't watch television or use the telephone until the homework is completed.
- Larry will receive extra privileges (going to the mall, inviting friends over to the house, and so on) if he gets his homework completed without difficulty.
- We will be more available to help Larry with his homework if he needs it.

Step 3: Share the List of Solutions

All solutions are accepted as being valid at this point and aren't criticized. This may be hard at first, but with a little practice, everyone can get the hang of it. Parents and children listen to all the possible solutions and, as in step 1, don't interrupt to comment or evaluate. The goal is to listen to all the alternatives in a nonjudgmental manner.

Step 4: Agree on a Solution

Now that the problem has been defined and a number of solutions listed, it's time to determine a solution on which everyone can agree. It's usually a good idea to have the child start by listing which of the parents' solutions would be acceptable to him. Larry might report that it's important to him to be with his friends after school and that he doesn't feel comfortable doing his homework before going out to visit them. He does like two of his parents' ideas: getting extra privileges for getting homework done and having his parents give him extra help with the homework. He's not at all happy about connecting the television or the telephone to homework completion.

When his parents review the options presented by Larry, they might indicate that they'd be willing to cut out the nagging but that they want him to do more than the bare minimum to pass. They're also not happy about the idea of Larry staying up later to get his work done. They agree to compromise about his friends but feel that homework has to be done before Larry watches television or gets on the phone with friends.

After further discussion, Larry and his parents agree to set aside an hour and a half each night after dinner for homework. His parents won't nag him, but they will be available during this time to help him if he needs it. Larry agrees to watch television and make phone calls after the ninety minutes devoted to his homework. Larry will also be allowed to go to the mall at the end of the week if he does a good job on his homework.

While Larry didn't get what he initially asked for, he was allowed to make his desires known to his parents and have them considered in a serious way. This process, and the sense that his feelings mattered and that his parents had clear and specific expectations, helped to set the tone for settling future disagreements. Having the opportunity to be heard in a serious way and see his parents make attempts at compromise helped Larry to be more accepting of their rules and less likely to defy them. His parents also had to stop nagging, give up more of their time for Larry when he does homework, and take him to the mall at the end of the week. Everyone won: Larry got some of what he wanted, his parents got some of what they wanted, and Larry was on the road to academic improvement.

Step 5: Implement and Evaluate the Solution

Making family agreements shouldn't be like making New Year's resolutions. Good intentions have to be actually carried out consistently for the agreement to have meaning. One of the best ways to review the status of parent-child agreements is through weekly family meetings in which issues of concern can be addressed. Each member of the family will have a chance to speak (briefly) without interruption. In this way, old concerns can be monitored and minor corrections made, if necessary, and new concerns may be caught at a time when it's much easier to take care of them.

Many families find that a good time to do this is at breakfast on Sundays. The important thing is to choose a time in which family members don't feel rushed, don't have to zoom off to a meeting or play date, and do have some free time to devote to talking and listening to each other as a family.

Parent-Child Time: The Benefits of Active Listening

Dr. Ginott also wrote about the need to actively listen to your child. Very often, a child doesn't have anyone to truly listen to her. One technique that I've suggested to parents with great success is what I call parent-child time. It's so simple that it may seem barely worth a notice, but it's one of those powerful practices that can be the cornerstone for building a strong bond between parent and child, for making a child feel heard and therefore significant, and for helping parents understand what a child is worried or angry or excited or happy about.

Each night, simply set aside between five and ten minutes in which you'll be alone with your child. The single rule is that only the child can talk. A parent can only listen, except for simple statements acknowledging that you've heard what was said. During this time, you can't criticize your child for what he says, give advice, or punish him. You're there simply to listen and let your child know that you understand how he feels. Having this outlet will help your child to lower his stress level and make it easier for him to deal effectively with difficult situations. The very act of talking out loud might help a child discover his own solutions to problems or help him develop a new perspective toward them.

If a child asks for advice, it's fine to respond in a nonjudgmental way that allows the child to continue to lead the conversation. You might say something like, "How do *you* want to deal with this?" Avoiding shock, punishment, or criticism will go a long way in keeping the communication clear and open. Even if the topic makes you uncomfortable (a discussion about drugs or sex, for example) you might say something like, "Do you want help with this?" And then it's critical to respect your child's response, reinforcing the notion that it's all right to talk about even very touchy subjects with Mom and Dad.

A Plan for Parents

▶ Adolescents are particularly sensitive to criticism. When things go wrong, don't attack your teenager. Dr. Haim Ginott said, "When a person is drowning it is not a good time to teach him how to swim," to which I'd add, "or criticize his performance."

▶ Write personal notes to your child. Focus on cooperation, rather than offering a negative critique.

▶ Allow your child to settle arguments by stating his case in writing, including recommendations for an appropriate solution.

▶ Use "I" messages instead of "you" messages. Focus on how you feel as opposed to what your child is doing. For example, try saying, "I feel upset when I'm nagged," instead of, "You are a pest."

▶ Allow your child the chance to save face and maintain self-esteem.

▶ Give your child choices. If he doesn't behave, then it was his choice not to comply and he must face the consequence that you'd discussed.

▶ Review your own reactions to your child. Don't keep doing what doesn't work.

▶ When a child is frustrated, she is not thinking clearly. Help her learn to think better by creating a map or script for handling things when she becomes upset.

▶ Practice looking at things from your child's perspective. Also, help your child understand how her behavior affects other people. Try role-playing exercises in which each of you takes the perspective of the other.

▶ Keep a log of the conflicts you have with your child, and note the outcomes.

▶ If you need to confront your child, keep it short. Ask your child if he can give you five minutes of his time. When the time is up, let the topic drop.

▶ Take breaks when you or your child is stressed out.

12

Behavior Management

FOR YEARS, PEOPLE have argued about which is the more effective motivator, the carrot (a reward) or the stick (a punishment). For a depressed child, the answer is pretty clear. Punishment doesn't work.

Why Punishment Is Ineffective with Depressed Children

The depressed child already feels as though he's being punished every day by his negative thoughts and feelings. If a parent thinks that punishment will teach her child a lesson and will prevent future misbehavior, she's forgetting that a depressed child tends to be future impaired. Her child is focused on his life being negative—in the short and the long term. He is irritable and has less energy to put into activities, which are of little interest to him anyway. A depressed child's negative behavior usually isn't a reflection of any desire to misbehave but is instead a reaction to stress. Your child may hit his sister or speak hurtfully to her because he is feeling irritable and has less control over his behavior.

When you punish him for this behavior, he focuses on *your* negativity toward him, not on his own negative behavior.

Too often, the child who gets the most punishment is the least responsive to it. She misbehaves, parents and teachers punish her, she misbehaves again, and the negative cycle, so hard to break, spirals out of control. A child who is frequently punished is a child for whom punishment isn't doing the intended job. Children who respond positively to the notion that parents will enforce certain consequences for misbehavior don't end up being punished very often. For them, the fear of punishment prevents the negative actions. But a child who is repeatedly punished tends to get desensitized to the process. Neither punishment nor criticism offers a child intrinsic motivation to behave and instead may lead to defiance and anger. The goal, after all, is to help a child learn to behave differently. Parents who get caught up in the punishment trap may have lost sight of this.

I've met parents who took all their child's belongings out of his room and withdrew all his privileges. Desperate, they sought my help because they'd taken away everything that could possibly be taken away, and still their child wasn't listening to them. My question to these parents has been, "Why should your child listen to you?" Not only is the child angry about his loss of privileges, he has no incentive to behave, since he's already had everything taken away. Makes sense, doesn't it?

First Reactions May Not Be the Best Reactions

Many parents resort to punishment when they're angry and upset, which means that their reasoning capacity is at its lowest level. If your goal is to teach your child, it's good to remember that you probably can't do an effective job when you're upset. A strategy that might help everyone is to say to your child, "I'm angry about this behavior, and I need to sit down and think more calmly before I decide what to do about it."

You may even encourage your child to offer input into the appropriate consequences for her misbehavior. However, keep in mind that some children will be harder on themselves than you might have been. You need to listen carefully and have some good idea of your own about having the punishment fit the crime. A child might say that she should be grounded for a month, because she is disappointed in herself and doesn't completely understand what it would mean to be removed from all normal activities for thirty days. Since she's living in the here and now, she probably won't realize the effect of a month's grounding until a few days have passed. My advice, then, is to let your child have input into the consequences, but don't let her impose an overly harsh sentence on herself.

Behavior Management, Not Punishment

Then how can a parent manage a depressed child's behavior, show him that his actions have consequences, and motivate him to want to behave appropriately?

The answers really lie in those questions! First, stop thinking about behavior management as punishment, and start thinking that your goal is to help your child learn to behave appropriately. Second, when he misbehaves, demonstrate that his actions have *reasonable* consequences that relate to the misbehavior. Third, provide him with incentives to control his impulses, complete required tasks, and treat other people and their property with respect.

The Goal Is to Teach a Child to Learn to Behave Properly

Punishment doesn't really deter misconduct, nor does it provide intrinsic motivation for a child to behave. When a child is depressed, punishment only serves to sharpen her focus on negative events, and this ultimately leads to anger and resentment. But please don't get me wrong—I'm not saying that you should give every depressed child a free ride. She still needs to be held accountable for her misbehavior.

The key is to look at discipline as a teaching tool and not a punitive tool.

I associate teaching with learning, and I associate punishment with fear and resentment. If your behavior management techniques are perceived by your child as being related to teaching, he'll probably respond more positively to your efforts. When your child does something wrong, the consequences should relate to what he did and should be in proportion to the misbehavior.

When you discipline your child, it's important to be consistent, clear, and assertive. For example, if your child is unprepared for school, the message you want to send is that schoolwork is important and there will be a consequence if he fails to meet the requirements. And as we saw in trying to resolve conflicts, the same caution about talking too much applies when you're disciplining your child. Some children are what I call parent deaf, a condition that is often the result of a parent talking too much, being overly critical, and going from zero to sixty at the first sign of even the slightest infraction of the rules. A child of parents who overreact might become talented at tuning out her parents' communications. And you must admit that if you were frequently criticized by someone who went on and on about your failings, you'd probably cultivate your tuning-out talent, too!

Most of us try to discipline our children the same way our parents disciplined us. Too often, we don't give thoughtful consideration to how to respond when our child misbehaves—we simply react and then hear the echo of our own parents' voices in the tone and the words we use. (This is probably true not only for parents but for educators as well.) We may feel that the more we punish a child, the more he'll learn his lesson and shape up. Unfortunately, the more you punish a depressed child, the more he's likely to withdraw and avoid behaving in the ways you want.

Once you get used to thinking about discipline as a teaching tool, I'd bet you'll be pleased at how effective this shift will be in making life with your depressed child more manageable.

Misbehavior Should Have Reasonable and Related Consequences

Sounds simple, right? But there are really two parts to this guideline. First, a child's misbehavior should have consequences. Again, this

---

Checklist for Discipline

Make a checklist to review when you are finished disciplining your child.

- Did you have good eye contact?
- Was your message clear and concise?
- Did you discuss positive alternative behaviors with your child?
- Was the consequence directly related to the misbehavior?

requires thoughtful consideration about what constitutes misbehavior, so that every action and reaction doesn't turn into a test of wills. A consistent response when the rules are violated helps reinforce the notion that a behavior is unacceptable. And second, whatever the consequences, they should be reasonable and not just a mark of a parent's frustration.

For a depressed child, it helps to keep the consequences to a single day. If they last longer, the result might be a deepening of your child's negative behavior and not the positive impact you should be striving for.

The second principle is to match the consequences you impose to the child's behavior. In order to ensure learning in the discipline cycle, it's important that the consequences of a child's misbehavior teach him something that will help him learn why his actions were wrong. For example, if your child has been hitting another child or calling her names, have him apologize and attempt to reconcile with the other child. If he's been stealing, you might have him return or pay for the stolen object and apologize to the owner. You might also have discussions about why stealing is wrong and have your child write a brief paragraph about that. If your child lies to you, work on encouraging him to tell the truth—and tell him that he'll suffer no consequences for misbehavior if he honestly tells you what he's done before you find out on your own. If he's willfully broken an object, have him pay for it, either out of his allowance or by working off the value of the object by doing extra chores.

Possible consequences for misbehavior include the following:

- **Loss of privileges.** Children who misbehave might lose privileges, such as watching television, playing video or computer games, riding a bike, going outside to play, or visiting with a friend. It's important that a child's loss of privilege has some connection to her misbehavior. If your child was watching television instead of doing homework, it makes sense to tell her that she can't watch television the next day until her homework is completed. If your child misbehaved when a friend was visiting, then she might have to wait two days before a friend can be invited to the house again.
- **Grounding.** Suppose you tell your depressed child that he must spend all his free time in his bedroom and leave the room only to go to school, have dinner, or go to the bathroom. He won't be able to watch television or play with games or toys or see his

friends. Sound familiar? Since this is the way a depressed child already spends his time, grounding is likely to have little impact on his future behavior. Save grounding for extreme acts of misbehavior, and limit it to a short period of time.

- **Time-outs.** A short time-out, in which a child is alone in a nonstimulating environment, can serve as a cooling-down period and can help a parent resolve a problem without the added burden of intense emotions. One major problem with imposing a time-out is that a child may refuse to go along with the restriction, but this is more likely to happen if the time-out is imposed for an extended period. The solution is to make the time-out short. Even if you send a twelve-year-old child to his room for two minutes, that's better than letting a situation get out of control. I've always felt that a time-out is an assertion of parental control and that the amount of time isn't as important as the fact that the child accepts that he has to listen to his parent.

  If you want to experiment using time-outs, it might be helpful to try the pattern that I've suggested to other parents, who have found it useful. First, make sure you warn the child that if he doesn't change a particular behavior, he's subject to a time-out. If he continues to misbehave, then send him to his room or some other nonstimulating place. Limit the time-out to one minute for every two years of age. If, after the time-out, he still hasn't stopped acting out, then you might try a double time-out.

- **Extra chores.** Some parents discipline their children by giving them extra chores. This might make sense if a child has broken an object and doesn't have the money to pay for it. The extra chores are a means of giving the child the opportunity to work off her debt. Piling on extra chores because a child didn't do her homework creates more problems than it solves and doesn't promote the primary goal of helping a child learn how to behave.

Provide Appropriate Incentives to Control Impulses, Complete Required Tasks, and Respect Other People and Their Property

Whenever you discipline your child, it's critical that you convey to her information about alternative behaviors, actions that would have kept her out of the hot seat in the first place. That's one of the incentives for changing behavior—*staying* out of trouble is much easier than *getting* out of trouble.

It isn't enough to punish a child. She needs to learn more about positive behaviors. This works best if parents (and other people around her) model the desired behavior. For example, if your daughter has gotten into trouble for using foul language in school, you might discuss other ways of expressing her anger. Instead of using a four-letter word, she can be encouraged to use words that are more acceptable. A little humor can help—I encourage children to make up their own nonsense words to express displeasure, such as *risp*, *blarg*, or *crents*.

When your child uses one of these strategies, a little praise or a small reward will go a long way toward reinforcing the desired behavior. After a while, a child is likely to realize that the way to get Dad's attention is by doing something right, rather than by doing something wrong.

Praise and Criticism Tally

Make a card with a list of praise and criticisms that you give your child for three days. Put a check in each column each time you praise or criticize your child. For example,

DAY 1		DAY 2		DAY 3	
Praise	Criticism	Praise	Criticism	Praise	Criticism
✓	✓✓	✓✓		✓	✓✓✓

Being Angry Doesn't Give a Parent Permission to Be Hurtful to a Child

Dealing with a child who has tested a parent's patience by repeatedly misbehaving can bring out some strong emotions. To provide an effective learning experience, though, parents should try to keep their communications calm, clear, and on topic.

Even when you're angry, it's important to talk to your child respectfully and avoid calling him names when you're discussing his behavior. Sadly, I know of many parents who call their children hurtful names when they're upset. Such labeling is likely to bother any child, but it will have an even more dramatic negative effect on the child who is depressed. A depressed child lacks the armor he needs to protect himself from negative experiences—he's more easily hurt. Name calling will stir up more anger on your child's part, which might result in an escalation in which your child replies with name calling, curses, and inappropriate language of his own.

Remember that it's the child's *behavior* that you don't like, not the child.

Try to keep your language positive, and avoid focusing on the negative. Children who are irritable and grumpy aren't easy to communicate with because of their high sensitivity to negative feedback. Once you make a negative comment, your communication may be effectively over. So try to avoid negative comments, yelling, and sarcasm. They don't work.

Explain things to your child in short, simple terms and avoid overexplaining. You don't need to go into a long analysis of why your child misbehaved—you may not even know why, but what you do know is that you want her to behave differently. And don't subject her to long sermons or lectures. Nobody, especially a depressed child, wants to hear a long lecture about her behavior. Tell her what she did wrong, tell her how she might have done it properly, and tell her what the consequences of her actions will be.

Strategies for Interacting with Your Child

Here's something to try that might improve your interaction with your child:

- Fold a piece of paper in half, and on the right-hand side, list at least five characteristics of the worst person you've ever worked with.
- Then on the left-hand side, list at least five characteristics of the best person you've ever worked with.
- Ask yourself which person you are most like in parent-child interactions.

Talk only about consequences that you truly intend to impose. Avoid threatening your child, especially using threats that you can't or won't carry out. Don't keep raising the ante by increasing the severity of your punishments if your child isn't responding. If you're one of those parents who has grounded your child for a day only to be met by defiance and shouting and crying, you might have been so frustrated that you kept adding time, until finally what should have been a one-day grounding ended up lasting several weeks. And then maybe you gave in after a couple of days because you realized you'd been too harsh. Better to avoid this scenario in the first place. Try to be as positive as possible and talk to your child in terms of consequences that you can both agree on, instead of being threatening and punitive.

▶ The Defiant Child

Cindy, an eleven-year-old girl, was referred to me by a psychologist who was treating her mother, Teresa, for anxiety and depression. Teresa mentioned to her psychologist that she was having trouble dealing with Cindy, who often ignored her requests and constantly fought with her.

Cindy came to the first counseling session with her mother, her father, Gerald, and her younger brother, Sean. Her parents' major issue was that she was defiant and complained frequently. She never did what she was told—instead, every discussion turned into an argument, and Cindy often engaged in the very activities her parents had specifically prohibited. When they told her to shut off the television or computer, she put it back on as soon as they left the room. She brought food into her room, even after she'd been told that she was allowed to eat only in the kitchen. Teresa and Gerald tried every punishment they could think of. None of them worked. Teresa constantly yelled at Cindy and hated herself for it. Her difficulties with Cindy made her think that she was a bad parent and she had a bad child. The entire family was in a negative cycle that they didn't know how to break.

Initially, Cindy didn't want to come into the counseling session. She stayed outside in the waiting room, tapping her fingers on the arm of her chair and scowling. I tried to avoid a power struggle with her and told her that it was all right to be in the waiting room and that I'd talk with her parents. Several minutes later, I invited her into the room so she could have some say because we were discussing issues that were of concern to her. She still refused, and I went back to her parents to discuss a behavior plan that we could use to reward Cindy for positive behaviors.

I wanted Teresa and Gerald to pay more attention to Cindy's positive behavior, rather than only responding to her negative behavior. Every day she might receive a point for meeting goals, such as complying with parental requests, doing her homework without a problem, and playing with her brother without fighting. If she earned enough points, she'd be rewarded. She might be the one to choose a movie for the family to see, be taken out for ice cream, or pick a restaurant for a family dinner. Once a point was earned, it couldn't be taken away. I didn't want to create a situation where Cindy might find herself in negative territory if she misbehaved. Also, I believe in creating family rewards in which everyone benefits from a child's improved behavior. Her brother, Sean, would benefit if Cindy behaved well, a situation that avoided the unfairness of Cindy being rewarded for the good behavior that Sean already demonstrated.

When the counseling session was over, I let Cindy know that she'd be getting rewards for more positive behavior and that no negative decisions had come out of the session, in the hope that she'd see that counseling could have a concrete benefit for her.

When the family came back for the next session, Cindy joined them in the room and we were able to talk. Sometimes an irritable and oppositional child requires a little extra patience. When we started talking, I realized that Cindy was extremely unhappy and had a long list of complaints against her parents and her brother. She now saw counseling as a place where she could express herself, in the hope that her family's attention might be used to help her.

We made steady and slow progress over the next couple of weeks, but significant problems still remained. Cindy had great difficulty accepting consequences from her parents, and her parents had difficulty getting out of punishment mode. Teresa and Gerald grounded her for getting a failing grade on her report card, so she couldn't watch television for a long time. They told her the grounding would end when her grades improved.

When Cindy wanted to watch her favorite television show, her parents told her that she couldn't because she was being punished. When they prevented her from turning on the television, she became violent. She threw a teacup and a vase against the wall and broke them, and then she started punching and hitting her parents. Teresa and Gerald put Cindy in her room until she quieted, but they were very distressed. At our next counseling session, Cindy reported that when her parents grounded her, she felt she had nothing more to lose. She had already lost all her privileges and had no incentive to listen to her parents or to demonstrate self-control. Her own anger frightened her, though, and she wanted things to change.

Her parents became more aware that behavior management needs to be administered wisely and carefully with a depressed child. Imposing a total grounding on a depressed child may bring with it a risk of worsening the depression or even inciting a child to violent behavior.

Discipline in School

Teachers, too, aren't likely to get good results when punishing a child who has an "I don't care" attitude. Schools vary in how they handle behavior management, and sometimes parents have to help educators better understand that a depressed child isn't likely to respond to the same kind of disciplinary measures as other children.

I know of one educator who left his position in a school because of a conflict over how the principal punished students. He was frustrated because the principal suspended students for problems without attempting to provide a solution for them. The principal asserted that suspension would be enough to solve the problem. That may be true of a well-behaved student who made a mistake. But it won't be true for a depressed child. Being suspended may feed a child's depression, causing it to grow and deepen because it removes her from the potential supports of social interaction. For a depressed child, who doesn't feel like going to school and isn't up to the demands of going to class and completing schoolwork, being suspended may be something she welcomes.

Instead of punishing the depressed child, we need to give him hope and incentives to improve his behavior, at home and in school.

A Plan for Parents

- ▶ Remember that your child's behavior is, in part, a function of how she's treated.
- ▶ Ask yourself if your disciplinary measures are really working. If what you're doing doesn't work, stop doing it.
- ▶ Don't be overly punitive. In my private practice, parents have expressed relief when I tell them that it's not effective to ground their child for several months.
- ▶ Try to take your child's perspective in order to be more sensitive to the way he's feeling.
- ▶ Don't decide on consequences for misbehavior when you're angry. Tell your child you need to think awhile before you decide what to do.
- ▶ Be impersonal while disciplining. For example, you might say any of the following:

> Chairs are for sitting.
> Blocks are for building.
> China is not for touching.
> People are not for hitting.

- ▶ Give your child the opportunity to fix his mistakes without you having to punish him. If he broke something, he has to fix it, pay for it, or work off the damage. If he hurts someone's feelings, he has to apologize. If he makes a mess, he simply has to clean it up.

13

Positive Communication

"Don't you know that the reports were due on my desk two days ago?"

"Where did you go to school—Mess Up University?"

"You have one more week to start improving how many cars you service or you're fired."

If your boss said any of these things to you, would they motivate you to do your job better, more enthusiastically, in a happier state of mind? I don't think so!

A child who has problems is sadly familiar with negative communication. His parents may yell at him or make disparaging remarks for failing to get classwork and homework completed. His privileges—playing video games, watching television, and so on—may have been removed. And he probably has to listen to his parents saying the same thing over and over, in his personal version of *Groundhog Day*.

The conclusion he's likely to reach is that his parents are terrible nags who are constantly on his case, or he's a total loser who can't do anything right.

His parents, on the other hand, are angry, frustrated, and worried. If they don't constantly remind their child, he won't do his schoolwork or chores. In this upset state, they sometimes lose control and respond sarcastically to their child, which only makes him dig in his heels and confirms his belief that nothing will ever make life better.

When it comes to people, there's lots of room for differences in behavior, but one thing I know for sure: nagging and sarcasm will have little positive effect on any child, let alone one who is depressed.

The depressed child is likely to have low self-esteem and often receives or perceives comments that reinforce that negative image. A depressed child is less likely to receive positive comments from the adults with whom she has contact than a child who isn't depressed. This negative experience might lead a child to become more defiant, disrespectful, and noncompliant because adults have come to be seen as little more than a never-ending source of negative feedback.

Parents need to work together to find effective ways to communicate with a depressed child, ways that are sensitive to the child's emotional needs. It's not enough simply to avoid the use of negative labels—parents need to learn and practice active listening and positive communication skills.

Sometimes we get so caught up in our own feelings that we're blinded to how a child feels about the negative experiences in his life. Most children want to do well and please their parents. Doing poorly is not a natural desire for a child. You need to believe in your child and treat him as he would like to be treated. Many children I've counseled, even those with severe emotional difficulties, have shown great improvement when a parent demonstrated understanding, communicated a strong sense of caring, and spoke in a kind and respectful manner.

Positive Support

Even though you weren't the cause of your child's depression, a positive relationship between you and your child can be a major factor in your child's progress.

Your enthusiastic support is a big part of helping your child move from depression toward happiness. I bet you remember saying things like, "Way to go, kiddo. Keep it up. We're so proud of you." You voiced your encouragement out loud, maybe even gave your child a big hug and rushed to get the camera so you could record the special moment. When the special moment celebrates a one-year-old taking his first steps, the child's parents are very excited and share their enthusiasm with him.

- **Celebrate victories.** Think of how good your child might feel if you could bring that same sense of excitement and enthusiasm to her in celebration of other milestones—some momentous, others marking smaller victories. Sometimes parents forget to share their excitement about their child's progress. This usually happens when a child gets older and her accomplishments are taken for granted.
- **Praise accomplishments.** You can share your excitement with your child by letting your voice reflect your feelings and by making comments that are directly related to your child's progress. If your child has just read a story aloud, you might say, "Mike, I'm so proud of you. That wasn't an easy story to read, but you pronounced those words wonderfully." Make specific statements that directly mention his accomplishments. Try to avoid saying, "Mike, you're such a good reader." If you don't mention the specific actions of your child (for example, pronouncing the difficult words in the story), he may not believe in your praise. Think of how you might feel if a friend complimented you on how you look. You'd want to know what your friend meant—did she like your clothing? your relaxed manner? the new hairdo?
- **Be enthusiastic.** Enthusiasm is contagious. It has an important effect on how your child feels about the goals she's working toward and the effort she wants to put into them. Acknowledging your child's accomplishments helps her develop a positive self-image and promotes good progress. Your enthusiasm and acknowledgment of your child's achievements help feed her desire to keep up the hard work of trying to reach a difficult goal.

You can't fake it, though. Your child will catch dishonesty, even if it's dishonest praise, right away.

Negative/Positive

Ask yourself how you feel when you get negative attention from others. Put yourself in your child's shoes, and write down how you think your child would feel. Then ask yourself how you feel when you get positive attention from others. Put yourself in your child's shoes, and write down how you think your child would feel.

Active Listening

Sometimes we don't hear what a child is saying because we're uncomfortable with *how* it's being said. If your child is yelling and screaming at you, you're probably not interested in the content of his message. Instead, you're focused on the disagreeable feeling that comes from being yelled at.

Rather than shouting back and turning a disagreement into a pitched battle, you might tell your child that it's hard for you to listen when he's yelling, insulting you, or using bad language. Assure him that you want to know what he's feeling, but let him know clearly that the message needs to be conveyed appropriately. You might tell your child to come to another area of the house so you can better listen to what he has to say when he speaks normally. By the time you reconvene, he'll have had a few seconds to calm down, and you'll be ready to give him your complete attention.

It's important that you give your child the opportunity to express herself without interruption and without fear of your reaction or of calling down negative consequences. Just having the chance to say what's on her mind is likely to help your child feel better and will eventually teach her that she doesn't have to resort to yelling or using bad language to get your attention. Your child will realize that if she acts maturely, she'll be heard.

Active listening is such a powerful tool that sometimes nothing more is needed to solve a family problem. By acknowledging someone's concerns, that person feels valued and may gain the confidence to participate fully in making a situation better.

Restating Is a Way of Saying "I Heard You"

One strategy used by good listeners is to restate in different words what the speaker has said or expressed. This is a way of checking that you really have heard and understood what's being said and lets a child know that you're really getting it. For example,

IF YOUR CHILD SAYS:	YOU CAN SAY:
I hate my teacher.	Your teacher makes you mad.
I don't want to do homework.	You don't feel like doing homework today.
This work stinks.	You don't like this assignment.

Communicating Positively

After you've listened to your child, acknowledging his feelings and working toward solutions may proceed more smoothly if you keep some principles of positive communication in mind.

Honesty Is Required

When you talk with your children, it's important to be honest and genuine in your feelings. Children have great radar for deception, and you can't hide your feelings from them. If you aren't honest, they will end up being distrustful and won't believe what you say.

"I" Statements Make the Point Clearly

If your feelings are negative, it's important to rephrase them in such a way that they aren't threatening. Dr. Haim Ginott suggested that people use "I" statements when directing negative feedback to others. Focus on how you feel, as opposed to what the child is doing. Instead of telling your child, "You did so poorly in school today," you might say, "I feel concerned when you don't do your best work in school, because I think it may mean something is bothering you."

Offer Specific Praise

Most psychologists suggest that when you praise your child, you should be specific in commenting on the particular behavior you like, as opposed to just praising his personality characteristics. It's the same principle as criticizing a particular behavior and not the whole child. If you praise by telling him that he's very good, you haven't given him much information that he can use. He needs to hear from you what behaviors he's exhibited that make you feel that he is good. He can't build his self-esteem on the basis of labels. Instead, his confidence will grow when he's acknowledged for concrete accomplishments.

If your child cleans up his room, it's much more effective to tell him that he did an excellent job of putting his clothes in the drawer, organizing his desk, and putting his toys in just the right place than it is to say he's a good boy. The same principle applies to praising anyone, really—if you write a good report at work, getting specific praise for your ideas about marketing a new product will enhance your sense of competency more deeply than if your boss just says, "Good report." The more specific the praise, the more useful it is for the child.

Look at Things from Your Child's Point of View

Make the effort to see things in the context of your child's life and the world in which she's living. It may be hard to admit or accept, but it doesn't help you or your child if you try to squeeze her world into a shape that matches your experiences when you were young.

The Temperamental Child

Some children are born with difficult temperaments. This idea has been discussed in several books. *The Difficult Child*, by Stanley Turecki, and *Raising Your Spirited Child*, by Mary Sheedy Kurcinka, present the notion that some children are born more impatient, more easily irritated, quicker to anger, or more intense in their reactions. An irritable child is a lot harder to satisfy than other children. These children demand more of a parent's time, and they usually get it. A demanding child can easily wear a parent down. Having a child with a difficult temperament can lead a parent to walk on eggshells in the hope that she won't do anything to cause her child to throw a temper tantrum.

In my opinion, the constant fear of a child throwing a tantrum may be worse than the actual tantrum.

If a child has always had a difficult temperament, it isn't likely that you'll dramatically change that. Focusing only on your child's temperament and attempting to change it will probably lead to more conflict and stress. It would be nice if all children were calm and patient, but perhaps this world would also be very boring. Instead of trying to change your child's temperament, your goal should be to help your child redirect her stress and assist her in making better use of coping strategies.

It's important to realize that a child with a difficult temperament may struggle mightily to control his anger and frustration. His difficult behavior may not be deliberate. Instead, he's predisposed to react intensely to situations he finds disagreeable or frustrating. This intensity may have little connection to anything you do as a parent. The key for a parent of such a child is not to fight against this intensity but to accept it and work with it and redirect it.

Try to accept the intensity of your child's feelings, and let him know that you're aware of his feelings. Also, keep in mind that intense reactions are contagious. As soon as your child becomes excited, you may also feel a rush of adrenaline and become very excited yourself. This can result in angry exchanges in which parents have a hard time keeping their cool. Counting silently to ten or warning a child that you're starting to get angry (which is also a verbal reminder to yourself) may be useful to help you get control of your emotions.

It's also important for parents to monitor what they say and how they say it to their children. Shouting and sarcasm are great ways to get a negative response, but they certainly don't help a child feel heard and understood. These reactions are a sign of parental frustration and may cause considerable harm to the parent-child relationship.

One of the most effective strategies that I've suggested to parents is to keep a log of how often they yell or make negative comments to their child. I ask them to create one index card for each day of the week and keep a tally of how many times they yell or make a negative comment. The very act of monitoring what has become a habitual response to a child helps parents become more aware of their behavior, which is the first step in changing it.

Communicating Your Expectations

For many parents, a negative attitude may develop when their child continues to do poorly despite the parent's best efforts. Sometimes a parent becomes frustrated when all his attempts to make positive change seem to have little effect. He has reached a wall and doesn't know what to do anymore. This may lead to a situation in which a parent develops "learned helplessness." It takes a special person to keep trying when his best efforts have been unsuccessful.

A parent's feeling that nothing is going to make a situation better may be due to unfortunate experiences that the parent experienced in her own childhood. A sense of hopelessness is passed down from one generation to the next, and it requires great strength to overcome the negative effects of a childhood in which a person was constantly told that she was "no good" or would "never amount to much." If you're a parent who tends to be unhappy and suffer from low self-esteem, you may find it helpful to visit a psychologist. The psychologist might help you explore your negative feelings so you don't pass them down to your children. Even young children are sensitive about the feelings of their parents and will be aware if they're unhappy and depressed.

Negative expectations for your child may also develop if your expectations are unrealistic and therefore can't be achieved. Imagine a father who wants his quiet, unathletic, scholarly son to be a star football player. That child will never meet his father's expectations—and parent and child are likely to become increasingly frustrated with each other.

It's worth spending some time evaluating whether your expectations for your child are realistic. It may not be realistic for a two-year-old child to always handle disappointment calmly and never cry out with a temper tantrum. However, it *is* realistic to expect that a nine-year-old will deal with disappointment without yelling and insulting her parents. Adjusting your expectations so that they're consistent with the age and developmental level of your child is part of active parenting. If you're unsure of what those expectations should be, you might consult with educators or mental health professionals, who can offer guidelines that will provide a reasonable range for each age and developmental level.

But the biggest reason that parents develop negative expectations is that they perceive that their child has established a previous pattern of not doing what he's supposed to and hasn't succeeded in making changes, despite their attempts to help. Some parents get frustrated when they try to get their child to put more effort into an activity and he doesn't respond the way they'd like. Parents may even go to the extreme of threatening and punishing their child. This strategy may work in the short run, but it rarely has any lasting power to change the situation. It also tends to damage the parent-child relationship and increase the child's level of negativity. Some parents take away all the child's belongings and privileges until she has nothing left, and still they don't get the child to behave the way they'd like.

Avoid Labeling

When parents have tried different approaches but haven't seen much progress, they are likely to feel discouraged. As a result, they may view their child so negatively that they end up seeing him as a "bad child." And at the same time, parents are likely to accept blame and may view themselves as "bad parents." You might walk around asking yourself, "What am I doing wrong?" Parents are then trapped in the blame and shame spiral. The negativity becomes a heavier and heavier burden that seems impossible to carry. If you get down on yourself when your child experiences difficulty, you'll end up getting sidetracked from the goal of improving your child's performance. Your blame and shame mind-set will get in the way of helping to turn the situation around.

I urge you to avoid the trap of labeling your child or yourself. Your child's behavior may be the result of complicated factors that are beyond your control. Once you apply a negative label, you prevent yourself from exploring other, more positive ways of approaching the situation.

Deliver a Consistent Message

It's important for parents to work together and deliver the same message to their child regarding expectations, goals, and values. However, parents may have differences of belief about how best to ensure a happy, healthy future for a child. This may be just as true for parents who are happily married as for parents who have experienced a bitter divorce. While some form of disagreement is normal, the important thing to keep in mind is that your differences shouldn't lead to destructive personal attacks, either on each other or on your children.

While venting frustration may release stress, by itself it doesn't lead to productive problem solving. Because the frustrations of dealing with a depressed child raise the stress levels in a family, parents need to support each other more than ever in this situation. The same principles I've suggested for communicating with your child may also be used in parent-to-parent coordination.

When children receive disparate messages about goals and values from their parents, the result is likely to be an undermining of

What Are You Communicating?

Ask yourself if you are giving your child enough recognition for her positive behaviors. Review the messages you communicate to her about your expectations. These messages might have a direct impact on her performance. Remember to communicate confidence in her abilities so she can believe that she can be successful. Leave taped or written messages describing how much you appreciate your child's positive efforts.

one parent's authority. Parents need to talk to one another about their child's problems and offer a unified representation of how they perceive the problem, how they will approach it, and what the ultimate goals and expectations will be. And they need to offer the same united front and back each other up in public. If you do have disagreements, keep them private and work them out, just the two of you, until you've forged a plan you can both live with.

The Power of Positive Beliefs

Your beliefs about your child have a direct impact on how you treat her. Our thoughts affect what we feel and what we do. If you believe that your child is lazy and ungrateful, you're almost guaranteed to treat her to a constant barrage of nagging and suspicion. If you believe that your child has a problem that hasn't yet been treated, you're likely to be more sympathetic and more willing to help her deal with her problem successfully.

If you don't believe in your child, he'll have a hard time mustering the confidence to believe in himself. Your beliefs will color everything you say to your child. If he hears enough negative comments from you, he'll soon come to doubt his abilities and he'll lower his expectations. And then your comments will have given him an excuse for continuing his negative behavior. If you tell him that he's lazy, he can now feel justified in not helping out around the house—that's not something lazy people do!

I've said it before and I'll say it again: if you take away nothing else from this book, I want you to believe that things can get better.

Nobody wants to have a negative attitude about his child. We all realize that negative expectations don't lead to positive results. I hope, with all my power, that the information in this book provides you with a foundation for developing a positive and realistic set of expectations for the children in your life.

A Plan for Parents

- Don't deny your child's feelings. Sometimes parents say things like, "Oh, come on, you don't really feel that way." Such reactions are likely to make a child less willing to share information and feelings with you.
- Try to acknowledge your child's feelings. Don't tell him that he has no right to feel that way. Instead, let him know that you understand how he's feeling. Acknowledging your child's feelings promotes a healthy emotional relationship and gives your child the satisfaction of knowing that he's been understood by you.
- Use a soft, calm voice when speaking to your child. Children often pay attention to the form of a message, as opposed to its content. Avoid yelling at your child, because the result will be the withdrawal of your child's attention.
- Let your child overhear you saying something good about her.
- Don't mix praise and criticism. Such mixed messages can be confusing to a child.
- Phrase your feedback carefully and positively. Avoid situations in which you only provide negative feedback—for example, "That's not the right way to do that." Cultivate positive teaching messages—for example, "If you scrape the food off the dishes first, the dishwasher won't clog."
- Be wary of all labels, even positive ones. If your child has a problem completing schoolwork, don't tell him that he's intelligent and imply that the work is easy for him. This puts him in a no-win situation. Instead, acknowledge his difficulties and listen to what he has to say about them.
- Ask yourself when was the last time you and your child had a good talk with one another.

14

Moving Toward a Better Future

IT WOULD BE nice if, as parents, educators, and health care providers, we could understand depression, learn about the best options for treatment, choose one, provide the ideal environment for success, cure all children and adults, and then move on to something else. But life doesn't work that way, and so our final topic is how to continue to move toward a better future. This is a journey that really doesn't have a final destination, because the future is always out there, beckoning with its promise.

What we can do is practice thinking, feeling, and acting in ways that reflect an optimism that directs our positive energies to continuing to work toward making things better.

Setting Realistic Goals

Part of the process of helping your child is learning to set reasonably realistic goals that you and your child can work toward with success. Taking small steps before you move on to big ones gives everyone confidence that progress is possible. You don't go from crawling to winning a marathon in a day or even a week. Your child isn't likely to be cured from her depression and start acting like a perfect child in a day or a week either.

Making your child a partner and working together means keeping your communication positive and respectful. It also means treating your child as a competent person who is capable of making progress. Optimism is contagious. Your belief that things will get better, even if it takes a while, is sure to have a powerful impact on your child.

Setting goals will help your child feel better and become more successful because it makes clear what needs to be accomplished, and the act motivates both you and your child to move forward toward them. Time and again, I've seen that a child will live up to the goals his parents have for him under three conditions. First, he must participate in establishing the goals. Second, he needs to see the goals as being relevant to his life. Third, he has to feel that he's capable of achieving them.

- **Your child should participate in establishing goals.** The whole process of creating a realistic blueprint for the future works better when a child feels he's taking part in establishing meaningful and achievable goals regarding his own behavior and progress. I'll discuss how to encourage that participation in an upcoming section.
- **The goals should be relevant to your child's life.** He may decide that certain goals that you consider important are, in fact, inconsequential to him. Sometimes when I discuss an exercise program with a depressed child, he'll acknowledge the value of the idea but then go home and not follow through. It's often easier for a child to go along with what you're saying just to end the conversation, instead of openly disagreeing with you. Whenever I work with a child to set goals, I tell him that it's all right to disagree with me. I let him know I prefer that he be honest with me and tell me that he's not willing to work toward a goal instead of telling me that he accepts the goal and then never puts a lick of effort into meeting it. Honesty is a critical component of goal-setting activities, and it helps to keep the initial stages of goal setting as stress-free as possible.
- **The goals should be achievable.** Setting goals that are unrealistically high will set you and your child up for failure. Having appropriate expectations for your child's progress goes a long way toward creating a calm and relaxed home atmosphere. If your

expectations are realistic, you'll have an easier time being patient with your child, who may be even more anxious and frustrated about his lack of progress than you are. When unrealistic goals are set, it leads to increased frustration and the possibility that both you and your child will give up on your efforts to work together.

A Workable Plan for Setting Realistic Goals

So, what are the ideal conditions for parents to get together with a child to set goals you both feel are legitimate and achievable?

- **Select a time and place to talk.** First, you need to choose a time to talk about goals. Your child will be interested in working with you only if the time is convenient for her, too. Let her have input into selecting the time, location, and length of a goal-setting meeting. She'll be a more willing and active participant in the process if she's had a say in the structure.
- **Give it some thought.** You can prepare for the meeting by letting your child know that you'll be thinking about some goals that you'd like to talk about and that she should do the same. This will allow her to feel that she's an active contributor in the problem-solving process and increase her motivation to put effort into getting better. A goal is so much more meaningful if it's chosen and not imposed. In order to come up with your objectives and goals, you should keep in mind a couple of things. We all have expectations of our children, but you may have to revise your expectations to take into account your child's depression and be sure that your child has the ability to meet your expectations at the current time.
- **Be aware of your own energies.** You also need to be realistic about what you can do to help your child—and what you can't do. If you put too much pressure on yourself, that pressure will filter down to your child and create stress in the parent-child relationship. You don't have to cure depression in a day or a week. You only have to take steps to improve your child's emotional well-being.

Sometimes, too, we expect a lot from our spouses and other children, so much that we set ourselves up for disappointment. Everyone has his unique stressors, and we may alienate other family members if we set up expectations that they cannot meet. The key to success is the same here: keep your expectations realistic, and set up goals that have a chance of succeeding. Lack of success tends to perpetuate itself. Small successes lead to more success.

- **Nurture your own positive attitude.** You can do a number of things that will help develop and nurture your own positive attitude toward your child. Most of these suggestions are designed to make you aware of things you probably already know but may have lost sight of in the daily challenges of living with a depressed child.
- Make a list of your child's strengths.
- Imagine yourself in your child's shoes, and write down what you'd want your teachers and parents to be saying to you.
- Keep a daily log of the negative comments you make to your child.
- Keep a daily log of the positive comments you make to your child.
- Construct activities that will help your child experience success.
- Listen to your child's expectations, and keep working to raise them one step at a time.

Long-Term and Short-Term Goals

When you think about what you'd like to see your child achieve, you might think about general objectives and specific goals.

General objectives are the larger, long-term goals that broadly define what you and your child want to achieve. You might create general objectives, such as feeling happy, not being tired, enjoying things more, or being less upset.

Specific goals are stated in the form of the particular behaviors that your child will be working to achieve. The great thing about specific goals is that they're measurable, so you and your child can readily see whether she's met the goal. But you both have to be clear about what the goals are. Make sure that you've reviewed the goals together and you both agree on them. It helps to write them down. Your child might agree to work toward such specific goals as sleeping through the night without waking up more than twice, recording one thing that she enjoyed doing each day, completing one day's homework in one and a half hours, talking about things that bother her without screaming, or exercising on the treadmill every other day for thirty minutes.

Resolving Differences About Goals

Most parents would like their child to share their own goals, but things don't always work out this way. Whenever children and parents don't share the same goals, the discrepancy may lead to stress and friction—but it doesn't have to. In my experience, one of three things may happen when people can't agree on goals or expectations. Somebody changes her expectations to go along with the other person, a new expectation is developed that everyone agrees on, or everyone agrees to disagree.

- **Change someone's expectations.** If you want to convince your child to change her goals and expectations, you'll need to find a clear basis that relies on her demonstrated abilities. Arguing isn't going to work, because people only change their expectations if they're presented with evidence that gives them a good reason to reevaluate their beliefs. If you're setting goals and objectives with your child, it's important that you call upon evidence that's based on concrete findings, such as test scores, work products, written reports, or clear observations of behavior.

    Opinions that don't have a foundation that can be demonstrated won't work either. Your child's therapist may prove helpful in resolving a conflict over expectations. Sometimes a neutral person can present information in a way that everyone is able to effectively understand.

    Parents should also be open to what a child has to say and be willing to modify their expectations if they're convinced by the evidence and the logic that they should be flexible.

Daniel was an intelligent thirteen-year-old boy who hated to do homework and in fact never did it. His parents were disappointed in his school performance, and they let Daniel know their feelings. Daniel had nothing against doing well in school. He would have been pleased if he had an A average on his report card. He said that he shared his parents' goal of his doing well in school, but he didn't share the smaller goals (doing his homework and classwork every day) involved in achieving those ends.

His parents decided they wanted to help Daniel change how he felt about completing his homework. They told him that he wouldn't be allowed to get together with his friends or watch television at night unless he had completed his homework to their satisfaction. Because Daniel had a history of being less than honest with them about his homework, they asked him to have each teacher sign a slip of paper indicating whether he'd turned in completed homework. His offhanded comment that he'd done it in study hall would no longer be enough.

Daniel's parents initially tried to change his position on homework by reasoning with him, but when reasoning was unsuccessful, they tried more extreme means. With restrictions looming, Daniel decided that it was in his best interest to get his homework done, and he accepted the goal of completing his homework every day. Ideally, parents should gain a child's cooperation in working toward a goal by reasoning with him. But when reasoning proves unsuccessful, parents may have to employ other methods to help a child see that it's in his interest to agree with the parents' goal.

- **Collaborate to come up with a new goal.** Sometimes the best approach to resolving differences in expectations is to collaborate and come up with a new common goal. Maybe the goal needs to be adjusted to take into account the need to achieve a smaller success. I think of this as the step-by-step approach to setting goals. Once the child meets the adjusted goal, then it's time to examine the next step toward eventually reaching the bigger expectation as everyone gradually increases expectations for future success.

Margaret, a nine-year-old with strong opinions, fought with her parents frequently over their desire that she read more. Her parents wanted her to spend thirty minutes a day reading. Margaret didn't feel that it was important to read every day. She didn't want to take away time from watching television or playing with her friends. No amount of talking convinced her to read every day. Because she viewed the expectations as unfair, she put even less effort into her reading.

Finally, Margaret's parents met with her to see if together they could work out a new solution and create a new goal that was acceptable for all of them. They asked her what she felt would be a reasonable amount of time to spend reading. Margaret told them that thirty minutes a day was too much, but she'd be willing to spend twenty minutes reading every day. Her parents and teacher talked about her compromise and decided that if Margaret kept her word, the end result would be much better than the current situation, in which she didn't read at all.

The fairy tale ending would have been that in two weeks, Margaret loved reading so much that she asked if she could spend an hour each day with her books. That didn't happen. After two months of cooperation, Margaret's parents met with her and told her how pleased they were that she'd met her goal consistently. They said that they felt she was doing better in school as a result of the reading program, and the improvement showed on her report card. Then they suggested that it might be time to try thirty minutes a day. Margaret, who was indeed pleased with her progress in school, still felt that twenty minutes a day was enough time for her to spend on reading, and her parents went along with her, since the larger goal of improving the quality of her schoolwork had been met.

- **Agree to disagree.** The least successful end to differences in goals and objectives is to have parents and child agree to disagree. It's usually better to try to modify the expectations and come up with a creative way of defining a new goal than to accept a disagreement in expectations. But sometimes parents and children may find themselves faced with just this circumstance. If everyone's participated by actively listening and communicating clearly and respectfully and your family is still having trouble agreeing on a goal, it may be best to acknowledge the reality of the situation and agree to revisit it at some future date. Engaging in active conflict may succeed only in pushing your child away from you.

Sometimes a conflict over goals and objectives is put on hold, with hopes for an eventual resolution. Peter, who is twelve years old, was just passing his classes. His parents wanted him to get higher grades, but Peter didn't share that goal. It hurt Peter's parents to see their son failing to work up to his potential. Still, nothing they tried seemed to matter, and Peter didn't make much of an effort in school.

Peter and his parents have different goals regarding his academic performance. His parents have, for the moment, decided to accept Peter's feelings, but they hope that they might come to influence him by taking a positive approach and encouraging him to do better. Peter understands that his parents would like him to put more effort into his schoolwork, but he feels so much resentment toward them for pushing that he can't—not yet. Peter and his parents have reached the point of agreeing to disagree.

This is one of those situations in which a counselor might be effective in helping the child and his parents move closer to common ground in their expectations. A counselor might help Peter discover the source of his resistance and help his parents become aware that if they want Peter's behavior to change, they have to change the way they approach him.

Maintaining Progress

After you've met with your child and come up with two or three reasonable goals, the job isn't over. You also need to arrange for ways to monitor your child's progress, and if you discuss this as part of a goal-setting session, then everyone knows what to expect. Using the good communication strategies you've been practicing—active listening, speaking without yelling, offering specific praise, and avoiding sarcasm, name calling, and global criticism—you should be well on your way to building trust and cooperation. Try setting a time each week to check in with your child on the progress she's making toward the goals. Offer her praise for specific achievements, and if she's struggling to meet one of the goals, give her support instead of criticism. You may need to reevaluate your goals and modify them, creating new goals that give your child a better chance of succeeding.

Three Helpful Questionnaires

Use the questionnaires on pages 228–231 to help you assess your family's situation and to assist you in monitoring progress. The first will help you focus on your child's strengths, the second will direct your attention to your own concerns as a parent, and the third provides a format for talking to your child about his feelings.

These questionnaires may be a good way to gather information to present to a therapist, or they can simply be a means to encourage a parent and a child to think in specific ways about a situation. Wherever possible, the answers should be written down. Filling out such forms periodically may allow for better tracking of a child's progress.

Continuing the Journey

It isn't easy to be the parent of a child who is suffering from depression. If I've done my job, then this book has given you hope and a belief that your child can get better. I've also tried to offer some insights into what depression is, how important it is to create and maintain a positive environment, and how you can develop skills and strategies to help your child make progress in fighting depression.

The journey won't be without bumps along the way. But I truly believe that with optimism, planning, awareness, and skill, your family will go a long way down the road to good health and happiness.

Your Child's Strengths

1. List areas in which your child shows strengths or talents.

   a. _____

   b. _____

   c. _____

   d. _____

2. Provide a concrete example of how your child has exhibited each of these strengths.

   a. _____

   b. _____

   c. _____

   d. _____

3. Under what conditions is your child most likely to show these strengths?

   a. _____

   b. _____

   c. _____

   d. _____

4. How often do you praise your child for his or her accomplishments?

   _____

   _____

   _____

   _____

Parental Concerns

1. List your major concerns regarding your child's behavior.

   a. _____

   b. _____

   c. _____

   d. _____

2. During what time of the day are these concerns most evident?

   a. _____

   b. _____

   c. _____

   d. _____

3. Describe a recent situation in which your child exhibited an inappropriate behavior that you are most concerned with.

   Define the behavior. _____

   _____

   _____

   What happened just before the child exhibited the behavior?

   _____

   _____

   _____

   How did you react to it? _____

   _____

   _____

What consequences did you give your child for exhibiting the
behavior? _____

_____

How did your child react to these consequences? _____

_____

_____

4. Describe conditions that make it more likely for your child to exhibit
   inappropriate behavior.

   _____

   _____

   _____

5. List strategies that have been effective in promoting positive behavior.

   a. _____

   b. _____

   c. _____

   d. _____

6. List strategies that have not been effective in promoting positive
   behavior.

   a. _____

   b. _____

   c. _____

   d. _____

Child Feelings Questionnaire

1. What problems are you having right now?

   a. _____

   b. _____

   c. _____

   d. _____

2. How long have you had these problems?

   a. _____

   b. _____

   c. _____

   d. _____

3. What do you believe to be the cause(s) of these problems?

   a. _____

   b. _____

   c. _____

   d. _____

4. What do your parents do that seems to make your problems worse?

   _____

   _____

5. What do your parents do that is most helpful with your problems?

   _____

   _____

A Plan for Parents

▶ Create conditions conducive to working with your child. For example, you might have a snack ready for the time you're talking to each other.

▶ Establish goals that your child has a reasonable chance of achieving.

▶ Keep a written record of the goals you and your child have agreed on.

▶ Give your child practice in achieving success. The more success your child experiences, the better he will feel because you'll be helping him build confidence and reduce anxiety.

▶ Once your child has gained confidence, you can modify the goals upward, in small increments. If the goals are too easy, they may not be interesting, and if they are too hard, they will make her anxious and depressed. Moderately difficult goals are the most motivating and interesting for children to work toward.

▶ Don't be afraid to vary your goals. Having the same expectations can become boring. Try to set up new challenges that your child can work toward.

▶ If your child cannot achieve a particular goal, then use successive approximations of the desired behaviors. For example, when a child is having difficulty sharing her feelings, you might ask her to share information about an event that day instead of a personal feeling.

▶ Spend more time emphasizing your child's strengths than his weaknesses. He needs to feel confident about his ability to be successful in meeting the goals.

▶ Acknowledge your child's progress, no matter how small it is.

▶ Praise your child for her progress as opposed to her effort. She won't pay much attention to your praise if it doesn't recognize real achievement.

Resources

Internet Resources

Organizations

Alliance for Children and Families
alliance1.org

American Academy of Child and Adolescent Psychiatry (AACAP)
aacap.org

American Association of Suicidology (AAS)
suicidology.org

American Psychiatric Association (APA)
psych.org

American Psychological Association (APA)
apa.org

Anxiety Disorders Association of America (ADAA)
adaa.org

Attention Deficit Disorder Association (ADDA)
add.org

Child and Adolescent Bipolar Foundation (CABF)
bpkids.org

Children and Adults with Attention-Deficit/Hyperactivity Disorder (CHADD)
chadd.org

Depression and Bipolar Support Alliance (DBSA)
dbsalliance.org

Kristin Brooks Hope Center
hopeline.com

Learning Disabilities Association (LDA)
ldanatl.org

National Alliance for the Mentally Ill (NAMI)
nami.org/youth/index.html

National Association of School Psychologists (NASP)
nasponline.org

National Foundation for Depressive Illness (NAFDI)
depression.org

National Mental Health Association (NMHA)
nmha.org

Suicide Prevention Advocacy Network (SPAN) USA
spanusa.org

Additional Web Pages on Depression

Defeat Depression
defeatdepression.org

WebMD
webmd.com

Your Depression Resource
mydepression.net

Bibliography

DePaulo, J. R., Jr. (2002). *Understanding Depression.* New York: John Wiley & Sons.

Diagnostic Criteria from DSM-IV. (1994). Washington, DC: American Psychiatric Association.

Edwards, V. E. (2002). *Depression and Bipolar Disorders.* Buffalo: Firefly Books.

Ginott, H. (2003). *Between Parent and Child.* 2nd Edition. New York: Crown Publishing Group.

Ginott, H. (1971). *Between Parent and Teenager.* New York: William Morrow & Co.

Greene, R. W. (2001). *The Explosive Child.* New York: Quill.

Ingersoll, B. D., & Goldstein, S. (2001). *Lonely, Sad, and Angry: How to Help Your Unhappy Child.* Plantation, FL: Specialty Press Inc.

Kurcinka, M. S. (2000). *Kids, Parents, and Power Struggles.* New York: HarperCollins.

Kurcinka, M. S. (1992). *Raising Your Spirited Child.* New York: Harper Perennial.

Morrison, A. L. (1999). *The Depression Source Book.* New York: Doubleday.

Naparstek, N. (1995). *The Learning Solution: What to Do If Your Child Has Trouble with Schoolwork.* New York: Avon.

Naparstek, N. (2002). *Successful Educators: A Practical Guide for Understanding Children's Learning Problems and Mental Health Issues.* New York: Bergin & Garvey.

Papolos, D., & Papolos, J. (1999). *The Bipolar Child.* New York: Broadway Books.

Quinn, B. P. (2000). *The Depression Sourcebook.* 2nd Edition. Los Angeles: Lowell House.

Seligman, M. E. P. (1975). *Helplessness: On Depression, Development, and Death.* San Francisco: W. H. Freeman & Co.

Stark, K. (1990). *Childhood Depression.* New York: Guilford Press.

Turecki, S., & Tonner, L. (1989). *The Difficult Child.* New York: Bantam Press.

Yapko, M. D. (2000). *Hand Me Down Blues: How to Stop Depression from Spreading in Families.* New York: St. Martins Griffin.

Index

sleep, 166–68
strategies for creating, 175
traumatic events and, 174–80
Swearing, 4, 201
Symptoms of bipolar disorder, 116–17
Symptoms of childhood depression, 4, 17, 19–20
Systematic desensitization, 109

Tantrums
anxiety and, 108
childhood depression and, 4
in preschoolers, 13
Roberta's story, 183–84
temperament and, 213
Teachers
discipline from, 205
feedback from, 143–44, 145
sharing information with, 76, 142
Teasing, 71, 177–78
Teenagers
Adam's story, 133–35
Billy's story, 3–4
depressed siblings, 158–60
depression in, 14–15
gay, 43
Greg's story, 172
Joshua's story, 161–62
mononucleosis in, 39
Roberta's story, 183–84
sex lives of, 93–94
substance abuse problems in, 111–13
suicide risk in, 42–46
Tom's story, 84–85
Tegretol, 122
Television, 4, 157, 179, 207
Temperamental children, 212–14
Thoughts, negative. *See* Negative thoughts
Time-outs, 200
Topamax, 122
Toys, new, 13, 153
Traumatic events
academic problems, 178–79
bullying, 14, 177–78
dealing with, 174
death of loved one, 175
divorce, 134, 175–76
illness or accident, 177

moving, 177
sexual or physical abuse, 10–12, 176
sibling trauma, 156–57
world and local events, 179–80
Tricyclic antidepressants, 92
Turecki, Stanley, 212
Tutoring services, 146–47

Unrealistic expectations, 214–15

Valium, 109
Victories, celebrating, 209
Video games, 4, 112, 170, 207
Violent behavior
Ben's story, 123–26
bipolar disorder and, 117
Brett's story, 127–28
Cindy's story, 203–5
hitting, 71, 117, 156, 206
Sam's story, 157
sibling conflict, 156–60

Walking on eggshells, 155, 213
Websites, helpful, 28, 233–34
Weight gain, 20, 93
Wellbutrin
bipolar disorder and, 118
for childhood depression, 89, 91, 95
Wellbutrin SR, 91, 107, 124
Wellbutrin XL, 91, 107
Wide Range Assessment of Memory and Learning (WRAML), 133
Wilens, Tim, 104
World and local events, 179–80
Worry chair, 168

Xanax, 109, 127

Zoloft
for anxiety, 109
bipolar disorder and, 118–20
for childhood depression, 8, 90
for obsessive-compulsive disorder (OCD), 111
in stories of patients, 8, 85, 101, 119, 128
Zyprexa, 122, 123, 126